THE CANADIAN DIPLOMAT

MARCEL CADIEUX

The Canadian Diplomat

AN ESSAY IN
DEFINITION

Translated by
ARCHIBALD DAY

Published under the auspices of the
Canadian Institute of International Affairs

UNIVERSITY OF TORONTO PRESS

The Canadian Institute of International Affairs is an
unofficial and non-partisan organization founded in 1928
and incorporated in 1950. As such, it does not express
an opinion on any aspect of international affairs. The
views expressed therefore in its publications are those
of the writers and not of the Institute

Foreword

BOOKS ON CANADIAN diplomacy are rare. The experience has been brief, the practitioners few, and not many have as yet retired to tell the tale. In accordance with the admirable custom of the civil service, Canadian diplomats remain virtually anonymous. Some, however, like M. Marcel Cadieux, by reason of their intellectual grasp, their academic contribution, and their dedicated participation in the life of the country gain a reputation in Canada and a merited respect abroad. Few men have done so much to enhance the good name of Canadian diplomacy as M. Cadieux, whose acumen, tenacity, integrity, style, and *esprit vraiment canadien* were justly rewarded when in 1961 he was elected to the International Law Commission.

It is fortunate for the Canadian public that this expert and experienced practitioner of the rare art of Canadian diplomacy has found time to write of it. His latest volume, *Le Diplomate Canadien,* was published in Montreal in 1962. It is addressed to young Canadians interested in a career in the foreign service and particularly to French-speaking Canadians. Its appeal, however, is to all those interested in the way our external service works. Because it is unique in its coverage and still more because it is informative, shrewd, and wise, the Canadian Institute of International Affairs decided to make it available to a wider public by publishing it in English. We have been able to do so with the assistance of the University of Toronto Press, of the Canada Council which provided for the translation, and of the translator, himself a diplomat and master of our two languages, Mr. Archibald Day of the Department of External Affairs.

JOHN W. HOLMES
*President, Canadian Institute
of International Affairs*

Contents

Introduction

THE CANADIAN DIPLOMAT is a servant of the Government who must carry out his duties both in Ottawa and abroad. With this definition in mind, I have tried to determine whether it were as yet possible to discover in him any distinctive characteristics.

The Canadian diplomat is a member of a young governmental service which has developed in unusual circumstances; work in foreign countries has an impact of its own, both through the nature of the duties and through the special circumstances in which they must be carried out. The profession has its own demands which leave their mark upon those who undertake it.

It seemed to me that in observing the peculiar characteristics of the Canadian diplomat I might find it possible to contribute something to two objectives which at the moment are of considerable interest. First of all, these observations might be useful equally to candidates at the competitive examinations and to officers of the Department of External Affairs in their reflections upon the character and the role of the Canadian diplomat; the usefulness of this project seems to me self-evident. In the second place, since a Canadian diplomat is representative of his country, the thought has occurred to me that we might apprehend through him, in the course of this analysis, an approximate image of a Canadian. I am well aware that to portray the spirit of a people, particularly of a young people, is an elusive venture; but if we draw enough sketches from different points of view, we may ultimately become more clearly aware of our national personality.

The era of purely material success must eventually give place in Canada to one of quite different preoccupations. We shall make little mark in this world if we continue to believe that our worth is measurable only by the sweep of the territories which our national sovereignty embraces, by the number of tons of wheat we produce, or, again, by the mileage of the railways we must maintain; now, on the moral and spiritual plane, we must search for and describe clearly, if we can, the face of Canada.

If I have succeeded in presenting clearly a portrait of our Canadian diplomat with reasonable accuracy, in demonstrating the principles which guide his conduct, in proposing, in short, some of the components in a definition of one type of Canadian, I will have made a contribution, however modest, to a study not restricted in its interest to a purely professional context.

M.C.

THE CANADIAN DIPLOMAT

1

The Diplomatic Service

THE CANADIAN DIPLOMAT belongs to a relatively new service which in its early years developed empirically; its first missions abroad had, like a flag, essentially a symbolic worth. The character of this service, the nature of its evolution, the present state of its development provide useful bearing points in our search for the definition of the Canadian diplomat. It is of course true that the contemporary Canadian diplomat no longer regards his task as fifteen or twenty years ago his predecessor was bound to do.

Our Canadian diplomatic service is new and at the same time old. If we are thinking in terms of a separate diplomatic service, ours, of course, cannot antedate the independence of our country. Even before Canada became an independent state, however, there did exist an organization to administer its external affairs; during the colonial period, and when Canada became a dominion, it was represented abroad—it still is for many purposes, as we shall see—by one of the ablest diplomatic services in the world, the British Foreign Office. The evolution of our foreign service begins, therefore, before Canada became completely independent. Many of its operations were at that time affected by our special relations with Britain, or by special needs which the Foreign Office was not in a position to satisfy. Later, our diplomatic service developed step by step with Canada's progress toward complete sovereignty. As with so many of our other institutions, moreover, the organization of our diplomatic service proceeded slowly, experimentally and by successive steps, not at all in accordance with a theory worked out in advance; its creation and its growth are closely related to the constitutional evolution of our country within the Commonwealth.

Confederation gave Canada independence in its domestic affairs. If it was not a sovereign state in international law, it was not possible either to put it on the same footing as ordinary colonial possessions not in full control of their domestic affairs. Its title, the Dominion of Canada, was kept for many years, even when it attained control in matters of external relations which could affect Canadian interests. In the beginning, however, it occurred to no one that the new Dominion might negotiate directly with foreign governments, or enter into diplomatic relations with the great capitals of the world. Furthermore, during this period Canada had no armed forces to give strength to a foreign policy which, in any event, it had no intention of working out in detail. London and Ottawa were in complete agreement: foreign policies did not lie within the competence of the Dominion. In these matters the Queen took decisions only on the advice, in London, of her Foreign Secretary; if the Dominion of Canada had certain claims to make, it could always let them be known to the Colonial Office which, in turn, forwarded them to the Foreign Office, if this were appropriate. In foreign affairs, Canada was a part of the Empire, differing in this respect hardly at all from the colonies. Canada was bound by international agreements of the United Kingdom; British diplomats represented Canada abroad, and protected Canadian interests.

If the new Dominion had little interest in diplomacy, it had, none the less, from its inception two important problems in the area of external affairs: immigration and trade. It had vast territories to exploit; it had to have immigrants to colonize and to develop the areas recently inherited, and, incidentally, to share the burden of the national debt. In theory, the diplomatic agents of the United Kingdom were to make Canada known abroad, and to encourage immigration. In actual fact, this system immediately proved to be impracticable; in Europe, as well as in the United States, agents of the British Government, more often than not knowing little or nothing about Canada, could hardly be convincing salesmen. Moreover, their first duty was to serve the interests of the United Kingdom, and they did not always have time or inclination to become advocates of emigration to Canada. There was the further point that in the United Kingdom, then one of the principal sources of emigration to Canada, the Foreign Office, like every Ministry of Foreign Affairs, having most of its officers abroad, could not readily stimulate people to come to make a new home in Canada.

Since the Foreign Office could not effectively resolve this special and urgent problem of immigration, Canada began to recruit its first officers for service abroad. A Canadian immigration agent was appointed in London in 1868, hardly a year after Confederation; a second appointment was made in Europe toward 1872, and a third in the United States in 1873. By 1903, on the eve of the vast wave of immigration, Canada had ten immigration agents in Great Britain, twenty-two in the United States and two in Europe. These servants of the Government had no diplomatic status, no special privileges of any kind, but they were the first distinct representatives of Canada abroad. Nowadays, their successors are attachés in our diplomatic missions, but are responsible not to External Affairs but to their own department.

These special measures, taken to deal with the urgent needs of immigration, soon became necessary in other areas. The growth of our population resulted in the exploitation of our resources; it soon became necessary to find outlets for the products of entirely new or expanding industries. As agents for Canadian trade, the British diplomats proved hardly more effective than in immigration matters, and for the same reasons.

There was, first of all, the problem of trade agreements. The British diplomats naturally were concerned above everything else with the interests of Britain; since they were often unaware of Canadian needs in any detail, or could be suspected of neglecting these needs when they came into conflict with those of the United Kingdom, Canada was by no means content with the results of their negotiations. Canada began by requesting that officers of the Foreign Office be accompanied by Canadian representatives when they had to deal with Canadian interests.

Later on, when Canada was not represented during the negotiations, a "Colonial Clause" reserved Canadian interests; Canada could accede to the agreement if it so desired, but without its explicit consent was not bound by commercial agreements signed by the United Kingdom. A further step was taken when, in 1907, Sir Wilfrid Laurier, accompanied by a few members of his Cabinet, conducted without other help negotiations for a treaty with France; the British diplomat came on the scene only at the last minute to sign the treaty with the representatives of Canada. In 1908, Sir Wilfrid Laurier sent Mr. King to Washington to discuss questions of Japanese immigration as a prelude to Mr. King's departure for London to advance Canadian views. This informal mission of Mr. King to Washington marked an important milestone along the way leading to the Treaty of 1923 in Washington which a member of the Canadian Cabinet, Mr. Lapointe (after certain difficulties raised not by the United Kingdom but by the United States) negotiated and signed. Thereafter, Canada possessed the right of making its own treaties, and for this purpose nominated its own plenipotentiaries. This same event established an important distinction between the interests of the British Empire, which rested with the Foreign Office, and the special interests of Canada, which were now protected by the Government of Canada and its representatives.

But treaties alone were not adequate to ensure Canada's commercial growth. Officers of the Foreign Office, as part of their duties, were expected to stimulate the sale of Canadian products. But the same difficulties arose; they had little knowledge of Canada or of its resources; their first loyalties were to other causes which could, on occasion, conflict with Canadian objectives. Thus there appeared once more a need for officers of the Canadian Government who could devote their energies as experts to the extension of our trade, to the exclusion of all other duties. By 1891, Canada already had eight trade officers abroad, one in Paris, two in Great Britain, and five in the West Indies. In 1892, in consequence of the establishment of the Department of Trade and Commerce, its officers abroad forwarded to it information on possible outlets for Canadian products; in 1893, there were thirteen of them who, although in fact businessmen engaged in their own affairs, also undertook to develop Canadian foreign trade; for this they were paid $250 a year. With the growth of our industries, this arrangement quickly became inadequate, and a professional trade officer was first nominated in Australia in 1895. In the course of the next few years, similar officers were sent to all countries which had commercial relations of some importance with Canada. Although having no official title, they had of necessity to deal with consular matters. For many years known as trade commissioners, these officers have now become consuls, consuls-general, and, in our diplomatic missions, commercial counsellors, secretaries, or attachés. Appointed by the Department of Trade and Commerce, they are members of the Canadian diplomatic mission, and they are immediately responsible to the head of mission.

For both purposes, immigration and trade, development has been identical: inadequacy of British diplomatic practices, an *ad hoc* and partial solution to look after our immediate interests, which did not raise, at least in the early years, any problem of principle.

As the Canadian services of immigration and of trade and commerce developed in Britain, it became necessary to co-ordinate their activities. Moreover, the new Dominion wished to borrow money in London; political questions began to arise, and a great deal of confidential information could no longer be transmitted in the official reports which the Governor General sent to the Colonial Office. Therefore, to direct the work of the many officers of the Canadian Government already in the United Kingdom, and to facilitate the conduct of its affairs in London, Canada appointed an official Canadian agent in London in 1874. A few years later, in 1880, his responsibilities were defined, and he received the title of High Commissioner. He had no diplomatic status; he represented the Canadian Government, not the Queen; but the prestige of those who held this post (one of the high Commissioners left London to become Prime Minister of Canada), and the importance of the affairs with which they were called upon to deal (as Galt in fact had expected in taking on this post in London) would later assure to them at least a quasi-diplomatic status. At the beginning of the twentieth century, the Canadian liaison officer between the governments of London and Ottawa held a position differing very little from that of a diplomat. The same development occurred in France: the duties of the agent-general appointed in 1882 were essentially concerned with trade and commerce and immigration; but eventually the agent-general became a minister, and later an ambassador.

Thus we see that well before the First World War, Canada, although having no separate diplomatic service, did have, in all matters concerned with immigration and trade and commerce, specialist officers at the important centres. In negotiations concerning the interest of Canada, Canadian representatives become the colleagues of plenipotentiaries of the United Kingdom. Finally, to co-ordinate the work of these officers and to protect its special interests, Canada maintained in London and Paris quasi-diplomatic missions.

In Canada, however, public opinion was beginning to grow uneasy. After the signature of the Treaty of Washington in 1871, and in consequence of the decision by arbitration concerning the Alaska boundaries, Canadians became convinced that British diplomacy too often sacrificed Canadian interests on the altar of Imperial objectives, and that the sovereign state of Canada should assume directly and exclusively responsibility for negotiations relevant to Canadian problems. The Canadian Government, however, proceeded prudently; the question at issue obviously bristled with emotional and constitutional complications.

It was precisely at this period that British statesmen were much preoccupied with the structure of the Empire. At fairly frequent intervals the representatives of the dominions met with the ministers in London at conferences, first designated Colonial (1897 to 1902), and later Imperial (1909), to study problems of common interest. The international situation was disturbing. The government in London wished to be assured of the support of the dominions in the event of war. Questions of federation and of an imperial parliament were in the air. The dominions, proud of their recently acquired independence, had no desire to be dragged into a war which might stem from foreign policies over which they did not have and could not have either authority or responsibility. Their co-operation, however, was essential in sustaining the crushing burden of military preparations; and there could be no doubt that they were beneficiaries of the peace assured by British military resources and diplomacy. Attempts were first made to associate the dominions in working out common foreign policies and in plans for the defence of the United Kingdom. Various formulas for consultation were attempted: first, imperial conferences; then, the Imperial Defence Committee and, during the course of the First World War, the Imperial War Cabinet. The consultations, however, never went in depth into the problems at issue, and the decisions taken led to consequences which the dominions were not always prepared to accept.

Specifically, Canada refused to commit itself in advance to an undertaking to take part in imperial wars. Canada was not prepared to accept the view that in any or every circumstance its interests were identical with those of the United Kingdom—the lesson of the Washington Treaty was not forgotten—and would not agree to take its place in the ranks on behalf of the common interest, that is to say, of the Empire. In consequence, Canada refused to consider plans for a federation, for an imperial parliament, or for any kind of imperial secretariat or organization which could drag Canada into accepting ill-defined and unforeseen responsibilities. The conclusion was finally reached that the real matter at issue was to determine whether the Empire was to become a distinct entity, with foreign policies accepted by all the dominions, or whether it was in fact necessary to recognize distinctions between imperial interests on the one hand and local interests on the other, and to rest content with imperial policies limited to common interests. If the first principle were to be adopted, the dominions would have no need of separate diplomatic services. Naturally, their advice could be taken on questions of great import, even though it were difficult to establish adequate media of consultation; but there would be only one foreign policy which the Foreign Office would be trusted to make effective. Naturally, with Canada, for example, certain measures could be taken to meet particular requirements; but these separate arrangements would not essentially weaken the concept of unity and of imperial diplomacy. On the other hand, however, if the second solution were to be adopted, there would of course be consultation and joint policies extending over as wide a sector of the Empire as possible; but when local interests were sufficiently important, these would have to take preference; and the governments concerned, as sole judges in such matters, would themselves take the necessary measures to protect their own affairs. This solution implied, on a scale yet to be determined and likely to vary according to circumstances, separate foreign policies and, assuredly, separate diplomatic services.

Clearly, the issue was fundamental and it became a bitter fact of contemporary politics in Canada. Some, in general the nationalists of Canada, held out for consultation, for common foreign policies to the extent that this was possible, but at the same time insisted upon Canada's right to act independently, even in isolation, on every occasion advantageous to do so from the Canadian point of view. Others, the imperialists, as their political opponents dubbed them, held the view that the power and the prosperity stemming from imperial unity were well worth the sacrifice of a few local interests. They urged a common foreign policy, and in consequence were opposed to the creation of a separate Canadian diplomatic service.

The dispute continued over almost an entire generation, beginning with the South African War, and the proposed Canadian contribution to the imperial fleet. Finally, largely as a consequence of the war, and also, it may be, in large measure because of decisions taken by the chiefs of the Conservative party, the second solution prevailed. The Commonwealth became the successor to the Empire, as a free association of independent and equal states, willingly and consistently consulting one with another, but following their own particular paths whenever their own interests so demanded. There was now room for the development of a Canadian diplomatic service.

In the War of 1914–18 Canada played an important part, whether on the battlefields or as a source of supply. Canada's contribution to the allied cause exceeded, for example, that of many other allied countries. Thus the Canadian delegates to the Paris Conference took the view that Canada should take part in the deliberations and sign the treaties of peace. It was quite out of the question to treat Canada as a colony, and to refuse to Canada what was willingly granted to the other allies. One success leads to another. Having once established its claim to sign in its own right the treaties of peace, Canada, when the League of Nations was organized, desired to be one of the founding members. Later, Canada demanded the right to be elected to the Council of the League, and followed the same line in the International Labour Organization. Comparing its industrial resources with those of other countries, Canada was not prepared to admit that it could be excluded from the Governing Body on the grounds that Canada was not a fully sovereign state. A little later, Canada, together with other countries whose independence was not questioned, sent a permanent delegation to Geneva.

Resting its claim on the importance of its contribution to the allied cause, Canada demanded and obtained international recognition of its sovereign status. Within the League of Nations and the associated agencies, Canada became a legal entity, internationally accepted. Thereafter, no question was raised of the Dominion's distinct existence in the concert of nations. The modest office on the Quai du Mont-Blanc at Geneva was the forerunner of the Canadian delegations to the conferences of San Francisco and to the United Nations Organization.

Although the Canadian title to independent status was recognized within the League of Nations, it was quite a different matter when the question arose of unconditional diplomatic representation in a foreign country. This was more than abundantly demonstrated by the tempest provoked by the opening of a Canadian mission in Washington. As the years went on, relations between Canada and the United States developed to a point where the Foreign Office, acting as intermediary, was no longer adequate to Canadian needs. Canadians, moreover, were by no means content, as we have seen, with the manner in which British diplomacy had protected their interests in the course of negotiations with the United States. It was their view that the United Kingdom too often sacrificed Canadian interests to advance its own imperial purposes. Further, particularly since the beginning of the century, Canada desired to have more direct and speedier relations with the United States. The International Joint Committee established by the Boundary Waters Treaty of 1909 was already a milestone of progress along this route; it was no longer necessary to make a detour by way of London to determine boundary questions and other matters provided for in the treaty (see especially Article X). This treaty created for the first time a direct and permanent means of communication between the two countries.

Meanwhile, the War of 1914–18 brought in its train a development of great importance in this same constitutional area. As the conflict went on, problems increased in number and required speedy solutions. A Canadian War Mission was sent to Washington and set about its work without excessive concern over questions of constitutional procedure. At the end of the war, the mission was recalled, but its secretary, Mr. Merchant Mahoney, remained in Washington to expedite current business. Provisionally, he opened his offices in the Embassy of the United Kingdom, for everyone was convinced that it was impossible to consider a return to the slow and tortuous system of the period before the war.

Having secured recognition from the League of Nations of its new constitutional position, Canada proposed to the United Kingdom that a Canadian minister be posted to Washington. The Government in London, anxious to maintain the principle of imperial unity, suggested—and Canada at first agreed—that the Canadian minister be the second-in-command to the British ambassador. Thus, Canadian interests would be appropriately served, and no assault would be made on the principle of imperial unity. We were at this time, however, in the very midst of the controversy on separate Canadian diplomatic representation, and such a gesture implicit with the gravest consequences was not accepted without disturbing the political depths. The Anglo-Canadian agreement was announced in May of 1920, but not until 1927 was Mr. Vincent Massey appointed as Canadian minister to Washington. During the intervening years there was a change of government, and the Liberal Cabinet insisted that the Canadian Mission in Washington be entirely separate from that of Britain. There followed the Imperial Conference of 1926; later, the Statute of Westminster would confirm the constitutional results. The United Kingdom ceased to have any juridical authority over the legislation of the dominions. In diplomatic affairs, the dominions, now autonomous, were to have separate representation to advance their special interests. Thereafter, no further questions were left for resolution apart from the levels and the methods of consultation. The diplomatic post created in Washington, for which the way was cleared by the Imperial Conference of 1926 and the rights earlier acquired in the League of Nations, cut short the question of the right to foreign representation; there would soon be Canadian diplomatic missions in Tokyo (1928), in Brussels, and in the Hague (1939) and, from then on, anywhere, as soon as Canada judged that its interests warranted such establishments.

The history of the Canadian diplomatic service has thus developed in two periods. During the first, which lasted from 1867 until the beginning of the twentieth century, the Canadian Government was primarily concerned with adapting the British diplomatic service to Canadian needs. It associated its own specialized officers with British diplomats, or provided substitutes for them for its own purposes. As time went on, Canadian representatives came to exercise most diplomatic functions without, however, having either the titles or the prerogatives of diplomats. The second period began with the imperial conferences. At that time, Canada was surging toward full development. Its growing economic importance, its rejection of the concept of a centralized Empire united in its external policies, led Canada to claim, first in the League of Nations and subsequently in the world of diplomacy, the full powers of all sovereign states. The establishment of a separate diplomatic service emerged as a result of its economic development and of its constitutional evolution within the British Empire. In some measure, the Canadian public had good reason to hail the birth and the precocious growth of the Canadian diplomatic service as symptoms and as symbols of the country's maturity.

The history of the service to which he belongs throws an immediate light upon certain characteristics of the Canadian diplomat. He is still feeling his way, he is still working out his traditions, his concern is with the work to be done rather than with his own status. For many years, the very fact of his presence side by side with representatives of other countries asserted the steady growth of Canada's sovereignty and independence, particularly in relation to the United Kingdom. This symbolic role is still essential, but, as we shall see, our diplomacy must increasingly take up the burden of its own proper activities. The Canadian diplomat, like his British colleague, once his master and now his associate, is not so much concerned with theories or formulas as with results and with practical solutions. It must not be forgotten that although Canada has earned its independence, it still remains a member of the Commonwealth, and its diplomats have been moulded by Commonwealth ideals.

The Canadian diplomat is the representative of the Head of the Commonwealth; under this title, he maintains special relationships with the missions representing the same sovereign in foreign capitals. Throughout the world, wherever there are other heads of Commonwealth missions, the Canadian diplomat forms with them a team. Although he represents a sovereign state, he bears in mind that the members of the Commonwealth are not as foreign states one to another, and that their representatives in their personal relationships should make manifest the special ties binding their various homelands together.

It is thus seen that the Canadian diplomat is a member of a service still relatively young, which has been developed stage by stage for objectives which are at the same time practical and symbolic, a service which has retained some of the qualities of its early years; its distinctive character in some respects still remains in process of formation.

2

Duties

LIKE OTHER PROFESSIONS, diplomacy can be defined in terms both of its historic development and of the duties which it comprises. In this and in the following two chapters, therefore, we shall consider in detail the principal professional activities of the Canadian diplomat, attempting to determine the somewhat special direction and the personal quality he can give to them, thus revealing his own distinctive nature.

Abridgement, like translation, is to betray a little. It is our impression, however, that we shall not oversimplify the essential duties of a diplomat when we recall that he is, first of all, the adviser to the Government on the consequences of its decisions in foreign affairs and on the effects which international events, or decisions taken by foreign states, can have upon Canada; in the second place, the diplomat has a special responsibility to protect the interests of his own country in foreign lands; as his third general duty, the diplomat must represent abroad his government and his country. The diplomat, therefore, appears, in keeping with the precise nature of his duties, as a specialist in international relations, and abroad, as a servant and as a symbol of the Canadian Government.

It is a commonplace to recall that nowadays, with the growth of rapid means of transport and of international trade, and with the vast increase in international exchanges of every kind, nations have become more closely linked one with another. To Canada, with its vast international commerce, nothing of any consequence in foreign lands or in the world at large could fail to be of interest. To discharge their duties as advisers to the Government on the course of world affairs and on the consequences of decisions taken in Canada or abroad, members of the Department must first of all be themselves well informed. Hence, it is necessary to maintain in the capitals of foreign states, and in those in the Commonwealth countries, embassies, high commissioners' offices, and consulates, whose duty it is to follow current events carefully and to prepare reports on issues or upon decisions which immediately or remotely may affect Canadian interests. If the Government of Britain, for example, proposes to reduce the importation of certain products, it is of the greatest importance that our representatives in Britain inform the competent Canadian service with all dispatch.

It is essential also to have in Ottawa services to assemble information which comes from all the capitals where we have diplomatic missions. This information is collated and, as need arises, presented to the Government to keep it fully informed, enabling it to make decisions in the light of established fact.

Since the establishment of the United Nations and of the North Atlantic Treaty Organization, many problems are now considered in an international context. The decisions taken are binding upon the various countries which are members of these organizations. To take an effective part in the work of these bodies, Canada must be able to send to their meetings delegates who can express the Canadian point of view precisely, and can protect the interests of this country. The Department of External Affairs provides officers trained in the work of representation and of negotiation which these international conferences or meetings demand. It is important also that instructions on the various items on the agenda be prepared for our Canadian delegates; the competent agencies of the Government must be consulted, and all important questions which might be raised in these conferences must be submitted in advance to the Government for decision. Canadian delegations normally set out for these international conferences with detailed instructions representing the views of the competent Canadian agencies and bearing the approval of the Government. Occasionally, delegates are given only suggestions or general instructions, since in some circumstances it is appropriate to entrust matters of detail to those who will be on the spot. But, in any event, Canadian delegates can take action only within the context of general policies already established, or as approved by the Government.

Every year, the Canadian Government sends an important delegation to the General Assembly of the United Nations. This delegation is usually headed by members of the Government, who are accompanied by advisers from various departments concerned with the matters which can come up for debate during the course of the session, and also by a team of officers of the Department of External Affairs. When Canada becomes a member of the Economic and Social Council, we must also send an appropriate delegation to take part in the deliberations of this organization; this is equally true for UNESCO, which holds conferences where Canada must be represented.

Thus, to transact our affairs expertly with foreign countries, whether with one country alone or in international conferences, there must be in Ottawa an agency to put together the information indispensable to the decisions of the Government which must be taken in our relations with other countries, or in the debates which naturally form part of international assemblies.

The Department of External Affairs is not only an information agency; this function in itself would be useful, but, in addition, officers of the Department have access to heads of government in other countries, and to influential men of affairs. Our officers do not merely gather together their views; frequently, when matters under discussion are of direct concern to Canada, our officers express the attitude of the Canadian Government. Quite often, these exchanges of opinion make possible a give and take on either side, a co-operation in negotiation which is profitable to both countries. The more accurately a diplomatic officer is acquainted with the objectives of his Department and of his Government, the more fully he is aware of local circumstances, the more capable will he be to fulfil effectively his duties as a mediator, as a go-between, and as a negotiator. It is apparent that what he does must be closely dependent on his awareness of general conditions in the two countries concerned and of the measures to be taken to put his case persuasively. In the following chapter we shall examine in greater detail the role of the diplomat as a negotiator; this, of course, forms part of his responsibilities in protecting Canadian interests or in making effective decisions which he may recommend to his Government, whether in commercial, cultural, or other matters.

The role of the Canadian diplomat is a curious blend of nationalism and internationalism. Canada's importance is not so great that its diplomatic officers, relying only upon their own resources, can produce a precise and complete account of everything going on in the world; the allied diplomatic services, particularly those of Britain and of the United States, often provide Canada with important means to reach decisions. With what our diplomatic officers receive from our principal allies, and with what they can provide themselves, they are able to discharge their first duty, to provide information, and to alert the Government on the significance and on the importance of current events. But it is also their particular duty to discover whether Canada's interests may be advanced, and by what method. In this, the elaborate diplomatic services of Britain or of the United States cannot make decisions for them. While attempting to assess the position of Canada in the flowing course of events, they may be able to perceive at the same time how this Canadian position may be brought into line with that of other countries whose interests are similar to our own. Our chances of influencing the policies of the great powers depend not alone upon our relationship with them, but upon the soundness of the commentaries we can put forward; and our influence can increase precisely to the extent that we can, on occasion, bring to light a policy corresponding not only to our peculiar interests, but also to the interests of other powers.

We do not claim that our diplomats attempt to express comprehensibly the point of view of the smaller or of the middle states, but to the extent that our officers are able to apprehend the interests of Canada, a middle power, there is a fair chance that the solution they suggest will be agreeable also to the points of view of countries whose position is in general similar to our own. It is evident, then, that our diplomat finds it doubly advantageous to regard general problems within a Canadian context; he is able thus to establish the interests of his own country and, on occasion, to ally himself with those of other countries of like importance. Furthermore, he can gain support and exercise an influence which could not possibly fall to the good fortune of our country acting in isolation. If he is motivated by an honest patriotism and if he is capable of giving well-tempered judgments, the Canadian diplomat not infrequently has a notable part to play.

A diplomatic service is not entirely preoccupied with negotiation, with the preparation of reports on international affairs, or with recommendations to the Government on questions that may be important in our external relations. A diplomatic service maintains missions abroad to protect our national interests.

Canadians, whether as residents or as tourists abroad, often do need protection, whether in a personal sense or for their property. The diplomat, as part of his normal duties, comes to their help. It may be a simple question of notarizing documents, but now and then he may render more important aid. A fellow countryman may be involved in an accident; if there are people injured or someone dead, very serious problems can arise. In such an event, the diplomatic mission will be extremely helpful to him; it can inform his next of kin, provide the services of a lawyer, make sure that normal legal procedures are being followed. Again, if citizens have property in a country abroad, the mission maintained there by their own country keeps a discreet watch to ensure that against such property unusual legal procedures are not taken. In brief, the diplomatic mission is a home away from home where citizens of the mission's country can get advice and assistance for any legitimate purpose. Those who have journeyed abroad and have got into difficulties—journeys and difficulties are often close companions—have experienced the ready advantages of being able to count upon the protection of their own country by seeking help from its representatives abroad.

Canadians abroad expect from our missions courtesies and services which representatives of other countries are not always called upon to provide. Ours is a young country, our traditions of hospitality are strong, and in foreign lands trustworthy relations between Canadians are readily formed. Our diplomatic officers abroad have in consequence somewhat special duties and, in turn, we find this tradition which is generally typical of our foreign service gives to it a quality which well reflects our Canadian practices.

Canadian diplomatic activity has in addition a representative function. Until very lately, it was fair to consider the Canadian diplomatic service as an organization still in the process of development. It is not for one moment suggested that the Department of External Affairs has reached the limit of its ultimate expansion; but it seems clear that its period of adolescence, of its precocious growth, will soon be at an end. No doubt new missions will be established, but taken together they will amount to only a very modest increase in the number which our country already maintains.

If the Department has, by and large, established its limits, it is on the other hand far from the completion of its organization; nor is it yet capable of playing its role with an easy mastery. It now remains for it to become clearly aware of its philosophy, to create its traditions, and to put its methods to the test. Most important of all, it needs time for its officers to gain experience, to acquire the easy skill permitting them to become masters of the areas of responsibility entrusted to them. As things now stand, the principal divisions of the Department are entrusted to officers who have barely fifteen years' professional experience. Their seconds-in-command, some of them at least, have had only brief experience abroad. Clearly, only with the passage of time will our diplomatic service be able to acquire full competence in the various areas of its activities, and to assert itself with the authority which should belong to it.

Moreover, for a long period, the growth of the Department of External Affairs was regarded as evidence of our country's newly won independence. Many Canadians, as noted above, found it an occasion for legitimate pride whenever the Government announced the opening of a new mission—the romantic era of the Department's growth. Now, however, External Affairs has become a part of the government service like other departments, a branch of the administration which justifies its existence by the practical services which it performs. The Department retains, of course, its representative role, but no longer, we are convinced, that affectionate esteem in the hearts of our fellow citizens in which it was unquestionably held at the time when our country was trying to establish or to assert its sovereignty.

Although in the earlier years, in the periods of the

Department's organization and growth, the Canadian diplomat had to be deeply preoccupied with constitutional law (his terms of reference were precisely relevant to Canada's degree of autonomy within the Empire), this period has now been followed by one of organization and of unification. The Canadian diplomat must now make use of his practical good sense in trying to discover the methods and the procedures most effective, most economical, and best adapted to Canadian interests. The business at hand is no longer to maintain an assertion now largely accepted—but to serve the taxpayer and the country in accordance with their needs, and at a reasonable cost.

Clearly, it is widely held that the Department of External Affairs enjoys an unquestioned prestige. Traditionally, the career is regarded as socially advantageous, and the diplomat as a person distinguished by very special preoccupations: elegance of appearance and correctness of manner. We would be the last to claim that nowadays, and notably in Canada, diplomats are scornful of protocol; but, if indeed it ever existed, the period when the diplomat regarded himself as a super-servant of the Government, a model of all the aristocratic virtues, is now long in the past; he has no longer any ambition to serve as a fashion plate. Increasingly, the diplomat has become a specialist among other specialists; he regards his duties as do all conscientious servants of the state; he wishes to serve his country by keeping his Government informed on matters which fall within his competence, giving assistance to his fellow citizens in countries abroad, and representing his country with dignity when called upon to do so.

Particularly through its representative duties, the

Department of External Affairs has been better placed than most others to appreciate Canada's advantages in possessing two official cultures. French Canadians have in consequence had the opportunity to play an interesting part in the brief history of Canadian diplomacy. Their Latin background set them apart in particular to serve as interpreters of Canada in the countries of Latin America and widely in Europe. In earlier years, Mr. Laurent Beaudry won distinction at the side of Dr. Skelton; upon this same road he was followed by a Désy, a Doré, a Dupuis, a Turgeon, a Vanier, and others who have won noteworthy successes in this career. Even if their duties required them to leave the Province of Quebec to come to Ottawa, or to pass a large part of their life abroad, their profession kept them in contact with the life of Canada in all its aspects; in the course of their duties as representatives and interpreters of this life, they become in fact not infrequently advocates of the values symbolized for them by Quebec, their smaller homeland. These leaders recruited in turn a company of young men, and each year the public examinations provide the opportunity to our young French-speaking graduates to join their number in a career both hospitable and rewarding to them.

Representing abroad a country which is new, bilingual, and one of the middle powers, the Canadian diplomatic service can from these realities now distinguish some of its special properties and characteristics.

In the following chapters, we shall examine the particularly delicate problems involved in promotions and postings in a foreign service which represents a country specifically both democratic and bilingual.

3

A Diplomatic Mission

EVEN PROFESSIONAL DIPLOMATS are not always able to
define clearly the functions of a diplomatic mission.
It is therefore not surprising if the public at large knows
only vaguely what diplomats do, when they are not
taking part in ceremonies or in important negotiations.

It is essential for our purpose to define the role of
diplomatic missions, since the work of missions and the
work of diplomats abroad are identical; thus may be
revealed some of a diplomat's essential qualities.

First of all, and very naturally, missions maintain and
develop relationships between their own country and the
country where they are established; they try to present
their own country in a favourable light, and thus, more
or less directly, to create if they can a feeling of goodwill toward domestic or other measures which their
Government may take.

A fine, vague answer, one might say, easily justifying all the undertakings of a diplomatic service, and its unlimited expansion! At this rate, countries should be represented everywhere, with hordes of officers; and national budgets would soon be overwhelmed through this desire to develop abroad sentiments of goodwill, which often could not result in any possible direct benefit.

This is a complex problem, as are all problems of relationships between two countries. The essential purpose of a mission abroad has been already suggested. In actual fact, this is not an isolated activity which diplomatic officers pursue for its own sake. It is rather an ideal which they must continually have in mind (here is the important point) while turning their attention to immediate objectives. For if diplomats do not remember at all times that it is their duty to create a good impression, the best possible impression, they can achieve no success in any of the separate day-to-day areas of their business. Moreover, precisely because of this underlying duty, diplomats are chosen for the qualities which will enable them to create an atmosphere of friendship and of goodwill.

Depending upon the countries, or upon local circumstances, the immediate interests of a mission may vary; but usually they are bound up in differing degrees with the development of trade, with the protection of the interests of their country or of their citizens, with the preparation of reports, and, finally, with negotiation.

But can the missions in fact be useful in the growth of commerce between two countries? There can be no doubt about it, and proof of this has been long established. Most missions have a commercial secretary or counsellor whose principal function is to find outlets for the products of his own land, and purchasers at home for what is produced locally. His diplomatic status opens many doors to him, and eases his task; the head of mission and the information attachés give him their support to whatever extent they find possible. The commercial secretary can take action immediately upon the introduction of a new protective tariff, and can protect or even guarantee profitable outlets for the products of his own country. He can inform manufacturers in his country of the organization of a trade fair, and make them familiar with the possibilities of local markets. In brief, in many different ways, the commercial secretary devotes all his energy to increase the volume of exchanges between the two countries and, in so doing, to strengthen the ties which unite them. Through commercial activities alone, the diplomatic mission creates an interest in and has an influence upon relationships between one country and another.

As is true for many other countries, the specialist in the commercial affairs of Canada is now no longer an isolated representative; he possesses diplomatic rank. And non-specialist officers of the Department in missions where there is not a commercial expert must be concerned with trade relations and with economic affairs. So far as Canada is concerned, the commercial and economic objectives are considered to be an essential part of the responsibilities of the diplomatic service. By force of circumstances, this orientation towards commercial matters tends to give to the activities of the diplomatic service a concrete, practical, and ultilitarian character which otherwise it might not have. The Canadian diplomat considers it his business to serve his country well in promoting its commercial growth, quite as much as in drafting political analyses.

It has already been observed in the previous chapter that diplomatic officers abroad must protect the property and the well-being of their citizens in foreign countries. In consequence, the missions must know the country well, since, to take useful action, they must know the country's institutions, its manners, and its influential citizens. And it is important that they warn the competent services at home on each occasion when the local government adopts a measure which immediately or ultimately can affect their national interests. These preparatory studies may have their purely academic side, but in fact are inseparable from the activity of the mission in this area as in all the others.

Diplomatic missions must also conduct negotiations. In this area of activity, an expert knowledge of the milieu, and cordial personal relations, can be decisive. A problem can be dealt with in many ways, but all of them are not equally advisable in all countries. The precise art of the diplomat consists in knowing when and how to take action.

Negotiations can be concerned with relationships between two countries or again with policies to be followed in the United Nations. By taking common action in the United Nations, two countries can sometimes achieve results which they could not possibly have attained acting separately. Questions of general policy also arise, and if a diplomat is equal to his task, he will find occasions to win support for measures which his country is advocating. In all countries, statesmen whose duty it is to make important decisions not infrequently find that they are alone and uncertain; at such a time they willingly consult the representative of a friendly country, provided they have confidence in his judgment. When countries have joined their fortunes in an alliance, for example, and when they must adopt common policies in perilous times, a diplomat can play an important role in bringing together or in interpreting varying points of view, by virtue of the knowledge he possesses of the character, the ideas, the misgivings of those who make the important decisions in the various countries concerned. To play this role, the diplomat, on such an occasion, must have the perception of a statesman.

The quantity and the nature of business to be done between two countries varies considerably; at some posts there may be enough to occupy the full attention of several officers. In other countries there are fewer problems, but even if during the course of a year only a few questions arise, it is no less necessary that at least one secretary devote his full attention to background study if he is to take action rapidly and effectively at the opportune moment. At times it may seem that diplomats are not in fact over-burdened with work; but it remains true that they must have the necessary leisure to know and to understand a country, so that on the day when they are needed, they are ready. Sir Harold Nicolson has rightly observed that at times a diplomat may have nothing important to do, but that he is there for the occasion when something important does happen. The witticism is an exaggeration, but does denote some measure, occasionally academic, of detachment and of study, which is an essential part of the profession.

Our own Canadian service has some difficulty in providing its officers with necessary leisure for study. The administrative duties which are normally more demanding in a new service require a great deal of their time; and administration has a particular tendency to acknowledge only tangible duties, easily discerned, and requiring immediate action. Canadian diplomats must devote an important part of their time to administrative work. They must, therefore, be adept at finding occasions, which their official duties do not always provide for them, to turn their attention to study, to research, and to reflection, which, it is undoubtedly true, in large measure contributes to the dignity of their profession.

One should perhaps observe in this duality of interests, some urgent, practical and tangible, others more theoretical but, it may be, more rewarding, one of the characteristics of the young Canadian diplomatic service. Its officers are not inclined to separate questions of principle from their practical affairs, or to neglect administrative problems because of their more theoretical preoccupations.

Simply to live abroad, diplomats must use a good deal of their time and energy in looking after themselves. There must be an accounting system and a consistent correspondence to maintain an office far from Ottawa. Even the smallest mission has inevitable staff needs. If the work involves various departments of government, the administrative staff increases proportionally. As we shall see in a later chapter, the preoccupations of the Canadian diplomat in this respect are probably somewhat greater than those of his colleagues in other departments in Ottawa.

The Canadian Government exercises a powerful control over its financial affairs. The demands of this control system do not always facilitate the tasks of missions abroad. This is particularly true since there does not exist within Canadian administrative services a wide experience of living conditions in other countries, or an established technique in dealing with problems bound to arise in the administration of a network of missions throughout the world. Ultimately, all these varied administrative snags will be smoothed down and greater flexibility will be possible. In the meantime, questionnaires must be filled out and authority must be obtained for casual supplies which the missions of other diplomatic services, more fully developed, can often deal with without referring invariably to the central administration at home.

If the diplomatic mission is to reach its objectives, its officers must make themselves known. The problem is complicated since it has been necessary to habituate the Minister of Finance to the notion that government servants abroad must have at their disposal salaries permitting them to entertain, to entertain well and often, to establish connections which may not be immediately necessary. In many countries this problem has been solved by accepting only the wealthy into the diplomatic service. In Canada, with its democratic traditions, this solution would have been absurd. Canada has insisted that its diplomats, quite independently of their private resources, maintain their appropriate position abroad.

The diplomat who takes up residence abroad to serve his country has no choice in the matter; he must make friends if he is to understand his surroundings and thus play an effective part. He has no common traditions or professional or family connections to introduce him to the people of the country; he must therefore ensure that the charm of his society, the attractiveness of his home, replace the customary background of relationships. We have already pointed out in an earlier work[1] how the

[1]Marcel Cadieux, *Le Ministère des Affaires Extérieures* (Montréal, Les Editions Variétés, 1949), pp. 46–48.

diplomat must take pains to analyze and to understand correctly the national ethos in order to serve his country effectively as its representative.

A criticism is sometimes made that diplomats hedge themselves in, within the diplomatic circle. It is of course true that diplomats, practising the same profession, are interested in the same problems and they have much to learn from one another. By exchanging their views and what knowledge they have, they increase their usefulness; the same holds equally true for their social contacts. It is at times difficult to establish relationships with the people of the country but through mutual invitations, diplomats pool and enlarge the circle of their friendships within the local society. In this matter diplomats are helpful to one another, generously and with goodwill, particularly to newly arrived colleagues. It would be unfortunate if this tradition should not be continued.

The diplomat, it was observed, must entertain from the moment of his arrival, and he must entertain on a generous scale. If he is to obtain the help he must have should the need arise, he must have a large circle of social relationships. Since he cannot know in advance what influential people he may have to approach, he uses his background knowledge of his posting, and knowing the nature and the probable extent of the business he will have on hand, he creates a network of social contacts. The margin of loss is undoubtedly great, to speak in financial terms, but this is the price of success.

Of course, there must naturally be a limit to expenditures or costs of representation. The minimum clearly depends upon local practices and on the rhythm of official life. Since our diplomats live in capital cities, they are members, so to speak, of a club whose conventions they must accept: official receptions, national ceremonies, high masses, and so on; all this takes time, it is often expensive, but it is unavoidable. On the other hand, a maximum expenditure can be fixed by estimating the volume of work entrusted to a mission. If there are frequent and complicated negotiations, if the mission must often take action to aid its nationals, if the policies of the country in question are of particular interest to the Department which in consequence requires frequent reports, clearly the diplomatic secretaries must maintain a wide circle of relationships on a continuing basis, and their expenses will be accordingly high. It is important to bear in mind that the costs of representation are proportionate to the results desired, and to remember the observation of Nicolson (many diplomats are inclined to forget it) that friendly relationships are not ends in themselves but means to attain precise objectives: trade promotion, broader knowledge of the country, easier negotiations, the protection of the interests of one's own country.

It must also be remembered that members of a diplomatic mission do not become skilled in comprehending the inner workings of a country by staying close to their offices. They must travel, must go to the theatre; they must read, and follow the debates in parliament; they must be on hand at important sessions of the courts, and they must meet influential people. All this takes time and, to do it well, very considerable resources.

All things considered, however, our representation abroad remains on a modest scale; there is nothing ostentatious or sumptuous about it. In the modest numbers of its officers abroad and in the manner in which they live, Canadian diplomacy gives a fair picture of a country which is prosperous but not extravagant. Our heads of mission do not live in palaces; but their rent is paid in advance, and their servants do not have to clamour to get their pay.

Together with representative duties there are also, as a means of extending the influence of a diplomatic mission, information activities. Particularly in recent years, with the refinement of media for publicity and for influencing public opinion, our missions are inevitably called upon to be concerned with cultural relations, and with the full run of governmental information activity.

First of all, requests for information of every sort must be answered. In this the missions have no choice and, in taking on this task, they direct their energies toward one of their principal objectives, to make their own country better known. Children in school want maps and photographs; students want information about scholarships; tourists want details on seasonal attractions and on particular points of interest; and often enough, in information activity, there is not much more to it than this.

The missions, however, can also take the initiative in distributing printed information materials, and films and photographs, which they have on hand. Rather than handing these out at random, they can relate this kind of activity to their principal purposes, and thus attain results all the more successful. If, for example, certain areas of the country are of particular interest for trade or for immigration, it is sensible to keep for such areas the first run of documentary films or the best of the available publicity material. Annual reports and technical publications also assist the staff of the mission to maintain good public relations, or to promote sales, quite as much as to create a general favourable impression, desirable undoubtedly for its own sake, but with results which are difficult to assess.

The missions naturally listen to short-wave broadcasts on their own international radio services, and give advice on the quality of reception and of programmes; they distribute government films and, observing the reaction of the audiences, may recommend different subjects. On important public holidays and other special occasions, officers of the missions discuss on the radio or in press conferences aspects of their countries which may be of interest locally.

Our Canadian culture has not yet a richness or a variety to be in itself a principal means of making our country better known. Our successes in this area are still modest, but our missions abroad take a particular interest in these matters, and are active in making Canadian cultural affairs better known within the limits of what they may do to emphasize the distinctive cultural qualities of our country.

Enough perhaps has been said to give an idea of the activities of a diplomatic mission; it is the instrument of one country's presence within the boundaries of another; by means of a careful network of relationships, our officers attempt to discover and to develop ties which can be formed between the two countries. Diplomats in some respects continue to be civil servants, but civil servants of a special kind; they must carry out their duties in conditions which impose upon them a need to be well informed, to serve with distinction, to represent their country appropriately; at home they would not normally bear the costs of these duties. Canadian diplomats must work with the modest means at their disposal, with limited leisure time, and with somewhat special administrative responsibilities.

4

The Diplomatic Despatch

IN THE PRECEDING CHAPTER mention was made of political reporting. The subject is of such importance that it is useful to analyse it in somewhat more detail; the studious work which the diplomatic despatch implies is basic to other diplomatic activities.

To a large degree the diplomatic officer is held in esteem in accordance with the worth of the reports which stem from his special knowledge of the environment in which he carries on his work. This is particularly true in the Canadian diplomatic service where an officer is hard pressed to find time for his despatches; his administrative duties and the flow of visitors conspire to keep him busy during working hours; and unless inspired by the sacred fire, unless urged on by a compelling need to analyse what he finds about him, taking this as the most profitable outlet for his energies, he can always discover good reasons to justify his inaction in this part of his responsibilities.

None the less, studious work and research which diplomatic officers abroad do or should do are of the very greatest value and importance; this becomes apparent if it is remembered that this work is directly relevant to the principal duty of the Department, to advise the Government on the consequences which events abroad may have upon us and, from the other point of view, on the effects which Canadian political measures can or could produce in international affairs. The advice of the Department is highly relevant to our country's alliances, to the risks of war, and, in direct consequence, to our national unity. It is thus essential that since its duty is to propose decisions in such vital matters, the Department be alerted on all the circumstances which should be taken into account. The same holds true, of course, for negotiations; the great art is to know precisely when and how to take action; and the most minute knowledge of the field of operations is clearly a prerequisite to success.

The work of political analysis, however, varies from mission to mission.

In the most important diplomatic posts (London, Paris, and Washington, and Commonwealth and NATO countries), the principal task is to reply to the daily questions raised by the Department. The officers who work in these missions must keep in touch with the competent divisions at home, and draft precise, detailed replies. Armed with this information, the divisional heads of the Department, keeping in close touch with other governmental services which may be concerned with the problem at issue, prepare for submission to the Government recommendations which, on occasion, entail grave responsibilities in financial or other affairs.

The larger missions do not provide only the information required of them; they maintain almost constant relations with statesmen and chiefs of the civil service concerning problems which form the subjects of day-to-day discussions or negotiations between Canada and the government to which the missions are accredited. Our diplomatic officers must then, following their conversations or their meetings (their normal method of work), inform the Department of the course of affairs. In many different ways, this work abroad leads to consultations which endlessly take place in Ottawa between the various agencies of government.

The Department also needs information on decisions taken or on events which have happened abroad, particularly if the consequences can affect our interests directly. This means that our diplomatic secretaries must watch constantly what is going on about them to decide, should occasion arise, whether Canadian interests are in fact involved. To prepare their despatches on such questions, our officers must maintain close contact with civil servants and others qualified to give them the exact, confidential information which they must have. In many countries, our officers get easily enough what they need. The governments and the agencies of the governments more often than not are quite prepared to co-operate with Canada to the greatest possible extent in resolving problems of common interest. But even in these countries our officers must have their own private bases of judgment, their own means of verifying or of checking; otherwise they would become nothing more than a means of communication, sending home blindly whatever they were told.

Whether the problems at issue are special affairs between his own country and the country where he is on duty, or whether they are matters of general policy, the diplomat is on the alert for the answers. From his post of duty, particularly if he is in a country of some importance, whether in absolute terms or in reference to specific problems, he can throw light upon certain aspects of the question and thus assist his Department in proposing to the Government the principles of a solution which may be acceptable and effective. To play his part as a skilled adviser, he must have a detailed knowledge of international politics and quite often of the intentions of the two governments.

In many countries, however, our missions do not have the task of maintaining so constant or close a relationship with the local authorities, and requests for information are less frequent. Even so, however, analytical and interpretative studies can take on considerable importance. In Iron Curtain countries, of course, civil servants and members of the government naturally have no desire to give us information allowing us to apprehend decisions of consequence for us, or to help us in the part we take, for example, at the United Nations. The patient studies undertaken by our missions in these countries ultimately provide us with a basis of knowledge which can give direction to our own views when called for, and can provide occasional useful suggestions on their practicability and on the tactics to be employed.

More often than not, the Department cannot give in advance detailed instructions on these matters. It must rely upon the good judgment and on the political good sense of its officers who determine according to the circumstances what events or decisions abroad should form the subjects of reports to the Government. It is therefore of great importance that our officers abroad have time to follow the course of current events, and enough training and maturity to apprehend what can be valuable to agencies of the Canadian Government.

Diplomatic despatches also presuppose on the part of our officers a long process of study, of consultation, and of co-operation.

It must not be thought that a diplomatic officer abroad has no difficulty in obtaining independent sources of information to check what comes to him from official circles. In the Iron Curtain countries the only method of testing official declarations is by personal observation, too often limited and at all times uncertain. In other countries this work is easier, but none the less still complex and time-consuming. To be successful, diplomatic officers must create a system of reference notes and files; they must read carefully newspapers and reviews, follow radio commentaries, attend lectures, pore over official documents and, in short, neglect no source of information, whether official or in the public domain. It is a vast field and the harvest is abundant; but even when they have diligently completed this task, our officers have by no means come to the end of their work. They must not concentrate upon studies of purely theoretical interest; in assembling their information, they must have time also to read the despatches and other documents sent to missions by the Department to allow them to follow what is going on in Canada; they must read Canadian newspapers and Canadian reviews to be familiar with changes in public opinion, and with the principal problems which the Canadian Government must resolve. Thus, they are able to distinguish what is of most importance to the Department and to use their basic information to prepare reports on subjects which can be particularly useful.

It is not enough, moreover, to prepare exhaustive information on subjects which can concern Ottawa; diplomatic officers must check their own conclusions; they must supplement them if they can to establish the precise substance of the problem. They request interviews with the most competent authorities. Sometimes they must try to get confidential information; at times it is essential to be closely informed on the intentions of the government; there is no published material and civil servants are bound to discretion by their professional ethics. At such a stage, the head of mission must take action to obtain the final complete details which only he can request. Sometimes there arises a very helpful co-operation between the head of mission and his associates; in fact, only to the extent to which the head of mission has been able to combine his representational activities with his own research work and with that of his subordinates can he put to best account the resources, necessarily limited, which are available to him.

Quite frequently, diplomatic officers exchange information with other members of the diplomatic corps who conduct similar studies on behalf of their governments; there are obvious advantages in their being mutually informed of the progress and of the results of their activities. On occasion they may share the conclusions of their various studies.

Within the mission there is also an exchange of information among officers belonging to various departments. The studies of the military attaché can often bring up political problems which officers of the Department of External Affairs can observe with interest. Political decisions can also have military or commercial consequences which External Affairs officers can usefully hand on to the military or commercial attachés.

It is equally essential that officers of one mission keep informed of the day-to-day work of their colleagues in neighbouring countries. For example, diplomatic secretaries in Bonn and in Paris are naturally concerned with problems of European integration. Clearly it will be useful for them to exchange their reports, and indeed to meet from time to time and to co-ordinate their work. Again, information and consular officers and the administrative staff can obtain, in the course of their work, information of the greatest interest to their colleagues responsible for following the course of political events; if they are alert to their duties, they will hand on such information to the appropriate officers.

It must be evident from these observations that the report, the diplomatic despatch, is the end, the synthesis of the combined knowledge of a mission and in consequence the beacon which guides and illuminates all its activities. A despatch is almost always the result of lengthy and detailed study; it presupposes in addition a measure of co-operation between the officers of all governmental services comprising the mission, between officers of neighbouring missions, and, on occasion, with the officers of friendly countries.

The number of despatches prepared by a mission naturally depends upon the interest and importance of local problems from the Canadian point of view. To accomplish this part of its work, the mission must keep informed of Ottawa's needs and must examine carefully local circumstances in all their varied aspects.

It is not surprising that only unusually gifted officers of the Department succeed in preparing useful reports. They must first be trained over many years, both in Ottawa and abroad; if they are overwhelmed by administrative duties, they cannot find time, and much time is required, to use their energies in this all-important duty.

It is quite wrong to imagine that diplomats can keep their governments adequately informed if they limit the information they send home to what members of the government can give them, or civil servants, or colleagues in the diplomatic corps. The drafting of despatches, it has been observed, is an exercise infinitely more creative, complex, time-consuming, and subtle. The merit of the Department as adviser to the Government or as an instrument of negotiation depends directly on the quality of the reporting which comes to it from its officers abroad and from the use which it is competent to make of it.

It would be an exaggeration to pretend that all our missions are of equal importance, but it is essential that the Department be sufficiently well informed to play its proper role on every occasion when a problem or an area of the world becomes of interest to Canada. Within certain areas or on the verge of certain problems, there may exist priorities in the needs of the Department; but there can be no doubt at all concerning the Department's need to have missions or officers numerous enough and adequately qualified to allow the Department to give to the Government advice comparable in worth to what the Government believes it must not lack in areas better known, if not more important.

This brief account of our reporting, the product of the wisdom, of the studies, and of the experience of our officers, gives us some glimpse of the qualities which by implication the diplomat must possess who undertakes it. This point will be raised again in following chapters, but it is already clear that an officer of our foreign service must possess a sense for politics, a thorough academic training, a well-established penchant for study, and at the same time a sound judgment of what is practicable, and an easy social grace—a combination of qualities rarely found in the same person.

The despatches discussed in this chapter are largely concerned with matters within the competence of the federal government; from time to time, however, affairs within the responsibility of the provinces, when relevant to general foreign policies or to federal problems, also become subjects of study for the Canadian diplomat. Precisely as did his predecessors in former years in the conduct of negotiations, he must constantly bear in mind the limitations of the powers of the Government to which he is responsible. Thus, the Canadian diplomat is subject to certain peculiar restraints: he is the representative of a federal state; consequently, in various circumstances his duties become especially sensitive and hazardous.

It is of course true that his manner of drafting despatches could not alone indicate the special qualities of a Canadian diplomat; but the individual worth and the personal hard work presupposed in the careful drafting of useful despatches, and the willingness of officers to co-operate one with another, are in this listing essential qualities which every diplomat must possess.

5

Postings

FREQUENT MOVING about the world is part and parcel
of a diplomat's life; the principles which determine the
postings of a Canadian diplomat can suggest to us a few
detailed points about his character—a few components
of the definitions we are seeking.

Officers of all diplomatic services are habitually witty
concerning the fantasies of personnel divisions in their
posting policies. You will be told in all seriousness that
if it is your wish to be posted to London, you must learn
Chinese and Spanish, to finish up in Russia. It is, of
course, unfortunately true that officers are not invariably
sent to posts which they would prefer and where, they
are quite prepared to believe, whether rightly or not, they
could be most useful.

None the less, the Department does consult officers
about their preferences; they are invited from time to

time to indicate their choices, whether for the missions
to which they would like to be posted or for the kind of
work with which they would like to be entrusted—political affairs, administration, and so on. The Department
is invariably edified by the replies; the vast majority of
our officers indicate their preferences for our posts in the
great capitals, London, Paris, and Washington, or for
work in political affairs. There does not exist a first-rate
administrator, often without any particular aptitude for
politics, who is not convinced that he could once and for
all reveal his true qualities if entrusted with a political
mission. In fact, the proposals made by officers are
evidence of the popularity and of the importance at-
tributed to certain missions or to certain kinds of work
rather than of their own native abilities.

Since the officers, as a general rule, are not remarkably
clear-sighted in the proposals they make on their own
account, the Department prudently invites the heads of
division or of mission to suggest in what areas officers
seem to have the best chance of success. Certain officers
exceptionally apt in consular or administrative work
dream of careers as economists, or as specialists in information. The judgment of their superiors does not always
coincide with that of the officers in assessing the most
effective way of putting them to work. Furthermore, if it
were necessary to rely upon objective judgments concerning the agents' particular aptitudes, they would rarely
find entrusted to them the particular post or the particular
kind of work corresponding to their desires.

In dealing with this question, the needs of the service
must clearly come first; we have a large number of small
missions scattered throughout the world, and for these
missions our particular need is for non-specialist officers

who can undertake administrative details and adapt themselves to all aspects of their duties. An officer who devotes
himself to protocol affairs in Ottawa must not be under
the illusion that he can continue in this specialty when
he leaves for a post abroad. More often than not, a problem of posting arises in a much more precise manner: an
officer, for example, is required whose language is French,
who holds a particular rank, and who has completed his
tour of duty in Ottawa. Since we have only 350 officers
in the entire service, and since about half of these are on
duty in Ottawa, it often happens that the choice is limited
to a single person, occasionally but rarely to two. Those
who most frequently are sent to the great missions are
naturally specialists in economics or in political affairs,
but so as not to favour them unduly in comparison with
their non-specialist colleagues and indeed in their own
interest, at one stage or another of their careers they must
be sent to the small missions.

   In our diplomatic service the officers, particularly at
the beginning of their careers, are not sufficiently aware
of the advantages to them in having a tour of duty in a
small mission. Whilst in London or in Washington they
usually continue in the same specialist work required of
them in Ottawa, in a smaller mission they must often learn
a foreign language, that is to say, they must at once
broaden their cultural horizon. In place of being isolated
in their specialist subject-matter, they must now turn their
attention to all the activities of the mission; and since
the mission at one point or another is concerned with
all the divisions of the Department, they can acquire a
much better perspective of all the different duties of the
diplomatic service. Moreover, they are called upon to deal
with administrative problems, and thus to learn that

problems in this field, just as in consular or in information affairs, are not marginal to purely political questions. This lesson is well worth consideration, particularly by younger officers. Finally, although in London and in Washington an officer can readily obtain what information he needs within the resources of the alliance which unites us with the United States and with Britain, in other countries he has much more difficulty in finding out what he must know. He begins an apprenticeship in certain of the more complex aspects of diplomacy, and he discovers the importance of personal relationships, and of warm hospitality; he discovers that all his essential information is not always obtained so easily as in Ottawa. And this will be useful to him when on his return to Canada he will be called upon to send instructions to those who have replaced him abroad.

In principle, officers return to Ottawa after each posting for a period of two or three years. Rather less than half of our officer strength is on duty in Ottawa. Every time an officer prolongs his stay abroad, he compels a colleague to remain for a longer time in Ottawa. Now, whether life is more agreeable or more rewarding in Ottawa than abroad, there remains the problem of ensuring that the advantages and the disadvantages of our service are equitably shared. Furthermore, all diplomatic services are afflicted by a kind of dichotomy; there are officers at headquarters who have not had much experience abroad and, on the other hand, there are officers who have almost always lived abroad and are not familiar with the difficulties which must be resolved in the capital, for example in obtaining financial authorizations. While officers at home accuse their colleagues abroad of living a life of ease and of making incessant demands, those

abroad complain, and too often with justice, that they
are not supported by their colleagues in the capital, or
that they are subjected to impracticable or unreasonable
demands. Through this practice of bringing officers home
to Ottawa after three or four years, however, there are
always at headquarters officials who have had recent experience of the problems to be resolved abroad; and
those who are abroad, having had experience in Ottawa,
understand how a request must be presented, the delays
which must be expected, and the limits of the reasonable.
So far, at all events, this practice seems to have given
excellent results. It has a further incidental advantage
in that it requires our officers, every three or four years,
to resume contact with certain hard facts of our national
life, in particular with the financial problems of their
colleagues in administrative duties at home; diplomats
who receive abroad supplements to their salaries for their
representational duties sometimes benefit from these
periodical cold showers.

The posting of French-Canadian officers presents
certain problems. Some of them would very willingly be
sent to Paris, and there live out their days. Incidentally,
the practice of rotational postings described earlier allows
a fair number of them to expect that during the course of
their careers they will do a tour of duty in the French
capital. Obviously, a posting to Paris gives to a French-
Canadian officer an additional training which can be
useful to him even from the strictly professional point
of view—all the more reason for not leaving the same
officers indefinitely in Paris, and for giving their colleagues a chance to benefit from this advantage. On the
other hand, if it is desired that French-Canadian officers
enter fully into the varied work of the Department, their
experience must be diversified so that at all levels and in

all fields they are prepared to make their proper contribution.

If the Department adheres to the practice of spreading French-Canadian officers throughout the service, certain consequences must be expected. First of all, in spite of the best intentions, they will not be represented in all the missions. We have about 350 officers. If about one-fifth of them are French-Canadian, that is to say about 70 to 80,* there will be only about 40 in service abroad since our officer personnel is divided about equally, as noted above, between Ottawa and the missions. We have 60 missions; if it is remembered that in Paris, Brussels, and in certain missions in Latin America we will always necessarily have more than one French-Canadian officer, it must follow that there will be missions where the French-Canadian element will not be represented.

Furthermore, in missions like Paris and Brussels, there will be not only French Canadians, and Canadian visitors will be unjustly indignant if they are not invariably welcomed by a compatriot whose native tongue is French. Clearly, French-Canadian officers would be by no means fairly treated if their experience abroad were limited to one or two special missions in Europe. Moreover, it is just as important that in other countries the dual character of Canadian culture be attested, by posting French-Canadian officers to the missions maintained there.

There must be no exaggerated insistence, furthermore, that the character of each mission or of every officer be representative of Canada; it is enough if the service in general properly reflects the essential qualities and the broad interests of our country. Although it is desirable that our officers know both languages, no one surely would claim that a Catholic could not represent the

*The Department is very anxious to increase this proportion.

Protestant element in Canada; an officer from Western Canada can speak for his fellow Canadians in other areas, and an officer whose training has been in the law can discuss agriculture. Rather than insisting that each mission represent each and every aspect of our national life, a manifest impossibility, it is more sensible to expect a reasonable arrangement: that French Canadians be justly represented in the service, both in numbers and in rank, and that the department in its procedures and in its policies bear adequately in mind what is considered desirable by the French-Canadian part of our country.

It is also of some importance, in comprehending the character of the Canadian diplomat, to emphasize the fact that the three most important of our missions are maintained in London, Washington, and Paris, where one of our two official languages is the local tongue. Thus, to get on with its work, Canadian diplomacy does not have to take on, as does that of Japan for example, the work of translation in addition to the very considerable task of understanding. We are associated with Britain within the Commonwealth, and we are bound to the United States by very close ties. From this it stems that Canadian diplomacy finds its task considerably simplified in its relations with the two countries which are most important to us. We do not have to storm the stronghold to gain an entrée; the special duty of Canadian diplomacy is rather to make certain that the two fundamental conditions of our alliance do not get out of their proper alignment; but since, so far at least, understanding with the United States forms the principal element of British foreign policy, to this extent the tasks of Canadian diplomacy are made easier.

It is equally impossible to comprehend the workings

of our diplomatic service if it is not borne in mind that several of our missions are directed by heads who are not career officers or who have never passed through the long stages of departmental promotion. Since the growth of our service has been rapid there have not been enough officers trained for the highest posts. While younger officers were learning their profession, the Government turned to the only possible solution by calling in distinguished Canadians who had already made their mark in other fields. In spite of their enthusiasm and intelligence, these heads of mission, having no background of common training, have displayed a considerable variety of professional procedures. French and English Canadians have emphasized varying aspects of the profession; but it is by no means sure that the variety of their techniques has not led to sources of detailed information which a staff, all graduates of the same traditional training, would not have been able to tap.

There is a further point; certain of our heads of mission have lived uninterruptedly abroad. Obviously, these have not had the occasion to become concerned with the integration of the work of our missions abroad and of the Department at home, or of constructing a general theory of the organization and of the functions of the Department. But in a service such as ours, where everything had to be learned from the beginning, those who formed the advance forces abroad did make an essential contribution, even if it must fall to others to complete it, and to contain it within a general philosophic framework.

The principles which govern the postings of our officers throw some light upon certain aspects of their inherent qualities. Because of our practice of rotation, our officers form a team. Again, our officers abroad do not lose contact with their homeland; and while in Canada, they keep in mind the idea of service abroad. Each of our officers, moreover, learns that he is not bound by the limitations of his origin, and that he must broaden his point of view to serve as an adequate interpreter of the aspirations and of the interests of our land, whose diversity forms its peculiar attraction. In his principal duties, an officer is not called upon to deal with difficult problems of interpretation confronting many other foreign services; his task is relatively simple. In consequence, the Canadian foreign service officer tends to resemble a civil servant rather than a traditional diplomat; and in cultural matters, he is strongly inclined to confine his interests to the two great disciplines of his own country; these give him the ability to solve the essential components of the problems which he encounters.

It cannot be claimed that all officers of the Department are bilingual; but within the service at all levels whether in Ottawa or abroad, there is a close collaboration, a continuous interchange among officers of the various regions of Canada. There are few departments of our Government where this association occurs with greater awareness. This continuing colloquy, begun and then continued throughout the entire career of our officers, is of great importance for our representation abroad. It may be even that it has also its own importance on the national domestic level.

6

Specialization

THE CANADIAN DIPLOMAT is not a specialist in any narrow sense of the term. He has retained very closely the ideal of the profession, to become an expert of a very special nature. He possesses indeed a variety of knowledge in a wide range of subjects, but he feels no longer any special loyalty to the disciplines of his university years; he is no longer a lawyer, an economist, or a historian. The question of specialization is important and must be examined since it throws some light upon the structure of the diplomatic service and upon its inevitable influence upon the intellectual development of our officers.

In all diplomatic services, specialization raises thorny problems. This question is relevant, first of all, to recruitment policies, since if officers are not expected to

be specialists, clearly the entrance examinations and consequently the candidates' preparatory studies will be differently ordered. Moreover, specialization has a bearing
upon promotion policies: in a diplomatic service where
promotion brings with it increased responsibility, it is
clear that unless specialists can move up to positions increasingly important and less and less narrowly technical,
their chances of promotion will be limited.

In general, there are two immediate solutions: that of
non-specialization, which so far has been principally
adopted by the Canadian diplomatic service, and specialization in an absolute form, that is to say recruitment
of specialists in law for the Legal Division, in political
economy for the Economic Division, and so on. Some
diplomatic services are more prepared than others to
allow their officers to specialize in disciplines for which
they possess unusual abilities.

The choice between these two policies is not determined entirely by theoretical reasoning. The general
structure of a service and its principles of organization
may incline it in one direction rather than in the other.
As for Canada, certain facts and certain principles must
be taken into account to explain its present policies in
this problem of specialization; even if it were possible
to question these principles, it would remain no less true
that certain clear facts impose upon us one choice of
policy rather than another.

The first fact which must be borne in mind is that our
diplomatic service is of modest size; the need for specialists cannot be so urgent as in other more developed
services called upon to deal with important matters even
within a limited area, as, for example, that of machine
tools in a particular country.

A second fact stems from the first; we have a few large missions, but usually our missions have only a very limited diplomatic staff: a head of mission, and a secretary who may be the sole Canadian professional diplomatic officer in the country where he is posted; if the head of mission is not a career officer, his second-in-command must undertake all the technical duties, and it is clearly not possible for him to think of becoming a specialist.

But we must also bear in mind the principle of rotation which has already been mentioned; our officers are called upon to serve alternately in Ottawa and abroad. The application of this principle results in making still more difficult any specialization on the part of our officers. This system has its disadvantages; it is expensive; it does not allow a diplomatic service the luxury of technical experts skilled in all aspects of a question, after their specialized studies of perhaps twenty years or more. But it does possess certain advantages. It does prevent this dreadful lack of understanding between officers abroad and those at headquarters, entirely ignorant of each other's special problems. If our officers spend their time alternately between Ottawa and abroad, there is a very good chance that they will be well-informed of the general policies of this country during their foreign service, and that they will have on their return to Ottawa a good idea of what their colleagues abroad can in fact do in accordance with instructions which may be sent to them. Our diplomatic service thus gains coherence, and its general effectiveness tends to grow even if officers in Ottawa do not invariably possess that expertise which a posting prolonged indefinitely in a country abroad would have given them. There are other reasons to support our system of rotation, but we do not need to labour the point. Enough has been said to give an idea of the principles and of the essential facts for an understanding of the solution arrived at for the problems of specialization within the Canadian diplomatic service.

It seems evident, then, that a diplomatic service of modest size, with its missions abroad limited in staff, and with its officers returning home every three or every three-and-a-half years, cannot afford the luxury of a large number of specialists.

But in point of fact, as the service grows, as questions become more complex, and as the need for continuity becomes evident, there necessarily arise pressures to make inevitable some degree of specialization. The precise problem is to determine to what degree these pressures must be recognized, and to what degree the acceptance of this need must influence recruitment and promotions.

Specialization, however, takes many forms. Thus, there may be specialization in regional problems; there may be specialization in functional problems. A regional specialist has expert knowledge of the problems, the culture, the history of a certain region—the Balkans, for example, India, or the Far East. A functional specialist is concerned with administrative, with consular, or with economic affairs. There is a further distinction; there is the officer who for years is preoccupied with the study of economic problems but retains none the less the desire and the knowledge to take on other duties in the service; and there is the officer who becomes a specialist on China or United Nations affairs and has no wish to emerge from the field thus chosen.

A solution to this problem has in the past been found readily enough by taking into account, above all, the needs of the Department; a beginning clearly had to be made with what the service required. It may have been theoretically desirable to have in the Department an expert in Arabic languages. The question at issue was to determine if at a particular moment the Department really needed such specialist knowledge. Circumstances might change, but the Department could anticipate and decide whether such an area of the world could become of sufficient importance to us to justify the employment of such an expert. The length of time allowed to the Department to make sure of its forecasts and to train its officers is precisely relevant to the difficulty of the subject and to the time required to master it.

As for its functional needs, the Department is well served by its present methods of recruitment. The Department requires a university degree; and its new officers normally have had adequate specialist training in one or another of the disciplines, law, political economy, or administration corresponding to the relevant divisions of the Department. The Department has no need to train lawyers; the competitive examinations provide enough of them, and as need arises they can be assigned to the Legal Division. The same is true for the economists.

This solution works very well for the functional divisions at lower levels, where problems are not particularly urgent.

On the middle and higher levels, however, the problem is quite different. Obviously, the head of the Legal or of the Economic Division cannot be an officer who, after receiving all his legal or economic training at his university and passing years abroad or in other divisions, is posted abruptly to the study of legal or economic problems—the most important and the most complex in the entire Department. For this problem the solution consists in leaving officers during the middle period of their careers, for five, eight, or even ten years, assigned to the study of legal or economic questions. The variety of their preceding training makes better specialists of them; and they have already taken their places as members of the departmental team. Problems simply do not arise which they cannot master, after ten years spent in the field of their preliminary university education. But they cannot remain specialists indefinitely for the simple reason that if they are to continue their progress in the diplomatic career, they must be prepared to take on more important positions as these become available; and whether they are called upon to become deputy or assistant deputy ministers or heads of mission abroad, they must then no longer remain specialists in any narrow sense. They must at this time be capable of apprehending a problem in all its varied aspects, a problem enmeshed in a net of complex circumstances, and in its relationship to the broad policies of their country. In other words, so far as the functional divisions are concerned, the problem of specialization is resolved by assigning to them for five or ten years officers who on coming to the Department already had university training in these fields. It can happen that they continue for even longer periods their work as specialists, as jurists, or economists in our larger missions.

The problem of regional specialists is somewhat more complex, and distinctions between one continent and another must be made. In Europe, in countries whose civilization is Western, in Latin America, in Anglo-Saxon countries, there have been no particular problems; our officers are educated in the Western world, and for them in these countries there is no great problem apart from language. A few months' notice in advance, the necessary allowances, a certain amount of leisure time in the mission abroad, and the foreign officer will readily manage to acquire the knowledge he needs. Whether an officer is sent, for example, to Spain or to Italy, he does not have to study a culture and ways of life which are completely foreign to him. No doubt he may have to improve his knowledge of the literature, of the history, and of local institutions, but he will already apprehend their general quality and essence. In brief, for most countries which are important enough for us to warrant an exchange of diplomatic representatives, our officers have already acquired the knowledge necessary to their work. There has been no need to recruit them in terms of their assignment to these posts; and they do not have to spend years and years in specialized study before their departure to these postings.

But for certain countries, even if our requirements could be determined or anticipated, the solutions indicated above are no longer adequate. To learn Russian, Chinese, or Japanese requires years of study; and to be an effective secretary in our missions in Russia, in China, or in Japan, it is not enough simply to speak the language; an officer must also be familiar with the culture, the civilization, and the institutions of these countries; and officers of the Department more often than not do not have the opportunity in the course of their university studies to become familiar with these parts of the world. This is equally true, of course, for the Near East or for the Balkans.

The problem, then, can be stated as follows: should experts be recruited with their training completed and with the ability to carry out the work of the Department

in these particular countries, or should officers be recruited for their general abilities and subsequently be
given specialist training? And, in the first alternative,
does it necessarily follow that these experts pass their
entire careers solely within their special fields?

When the Department has been able to foresee long
enough in advance a need for experts in a particular
country or area, it has taken care to give specialist training to officers recruited in the normal ways; and their
abilities have been well known to the Department. When,
however, unexpected needs have arisen, the Department
has had to recruit specialists from outside, requiring,
however, that these officers possess, so far as this is possible, the abilities normally expected of non-specialist
officers. For the specialist pure and simple does not become a diplomat; he has no career to look forward to.
He is limited to one or two missions, always the same
missions; and there is no great future for him.

It is conceivable that Tibet may some day become a
country important to Canada; the expert familiar with
its problems could in time become secretary of the mission we would have there, but he could scarcely rise in
rank in Ottawa except to the extent of his ability to deal
with much broader questions—that is to say to the point
where he would in fact no longer be a Tibetan specialist.
The solution of this problem so far has been bound up
with the Department's ability to estimate its needs accurately, and to train as specialists officers who have
already demonstrated their competence in other ways.

But has it in fact been necessary to confine these experts within the limited field of their specialization? This,
as we have observed, would put an end to their chances
of promotion; but in addition interests of the service

would have to be sacrificed. Just as it has been essential to strengthen ties between officers abroad and officers in Ottawa by giving them alternating postings, so it has been necessary to establish certain regional relationships; it is to the advantage of the specialist in European questions to have a tour of duty, at some stage of his career, in Asia or in South America. This has been equally true for the expert in Chinese or Japanese affairs; he has profited from a tour of duty in Moscow. This policy has presupposed, however, the existence of officers trained by the department to serve as relief officers. The exercise has been somewhat more complex than in the functional divisions, but the principle has remained the same: no specialists to begin with; after a generalist period, longer or shorter according to the difficulty of the subject proposed, specialization, but not for an indefinite period. The specialist officer has returned to problems of general policy; but it has been necessary, of course, to make provision for his departure, and to make certain of a successor to him.

From all of this it becomes evident that the diplomat, as a diplomat, is already a specialist in a certain limited sense. Officers whose university training has been in law or economics, who have completed their apprenticeship, and who have not been posted to the Legal or Economic Division, learn the skills and the right ordering of a genuine profession. They are initiated into the arts of negotiation; they become experts in drafting despatches; they are skilled in the operations of the Department, or of a post abroad; this is the field of their studies, the area of their specialization. From one area of the world to another, from one problem to another, the essentials of the techniques remain identical; and problems which in certain countries may appear to be insuperable can in fact be mastered after a few years of applied effort. By refusing to get involved in a mania for specialization which would have been as useless for the Department as prejudicial to the essential quality of the profession, the Department has avoided distorting the good management of the service and endangering the nice balance of its officer cadre.

Fundamentally, therefore, the rather sparse complement of the Canadian diplomatic service is an obstacle to excessive specialization on the part of its officers. And this is all to the good; our officers thus remain faithful to the spirit of the profession, to the ideal of the honourable man of varied abilities and interests who makes it his duty to apply himself to all aspects of Canadian life that he may represent it abroad with the diversity of resources which is the very essence of his profession.

7

Recruitment

THE COMPETITIVE EXAMINATION for admission to the
Department of External Affairs is reputed to be difficult,
and justly so. The diplomatic career is attractive, and
the Department is quite right in choosing with the
greatest care its new officers from the large number of
candidates. However, and this is important for those
who are preparing for the competition, the methods
adopted by the Department to determine its choices are
not capriciously subjective, and they suggest the scale
of values which for its purposes the Department has set.
To renew its ranks, the Department has had to make a
conscious effort of self-examination on the precise design
which is the purpose of this part of our study.

Before announcing a public competition, the responsible officers within the Department and the Civil Service

Commission undertake a very careful study of the qualities and of the skills essential to young secretaries. In
brief, the Department and the Commission consider this
question: "What kind of young man do we wish to choose
as an officer of Canada's foreign service?"

The classic texts on the diplomat (Cambon, Nicolson, Jusserand, d'Ormesson, de Szilassy) naturally throw
some light on his qualities as a man and as an individual,
but are not particularly useful in defining the technical
abilities and the precise funds of knowledge which the
secretary of an embassy needs for the proper practice of
his trade.

All authorities are in full agreement in underlining
the importance of moral and personal worth. Nicolson
and Cambon, in particular, make a careful study of these
qualities, and in their view, as is well known, a good
diplomat must have the virtues of exactness, of calm, of
patience, of modesty, of integrity, and so on. This list,
however, is not adequate. It must also be asked whether
young diplomats do not need a special education and,
further, what disciplines seem to offer the best preparation for a diplomatic career.

Jusserand, in his *Ecole des Ambassadeurs,* is more
exact. He made a study of what the authorities over the
centuries have considered to be the most useful funds
of knowledge which a diplomat should possess to be
successful. Writers of the Renaissance held the view that
an ambassador must possess practically limitless knowledge. Sir Thomas More, in his *Utopia,* wrote that ambassadors are chosen, as are priests, from among learned
citizens. According to Hotmann, another authority of
the same period, an ambassador had to be an insatiable
reader. His own particular interest was in history; on

this point his contemporary authorities were unanimous; but according to Jusserand history was only one part of the encyclopaedic knowledge which an ambassador must possess. He must be learned in the Bible, in the sciences, in politics, in geography, in the military arts, and in philosophy. Further, writers of the Renaissance believed that a good diplomat should know not only the various regions of the world, but music as well, and then even considered that he must find time to spend in contemplative thought. As a matter of course, a diplomat had to speak several foreign languages, be an expert in Roman law, and find means to become a good writer.

In the seventeenth century, Rousseau de Chancy observed that a diplomat should be prepared, if need arose, to ask for new instructions; lacking instructions, he must know how to act with good sense and to take opportune action to protect the interests of his country. It seemed to him that a diplomat must be something more than an ordinary postman, forwarding to his own or to a foreign government despatches relevant to the common interest of the two countries.

Jusserand described in detail the organization of a school of diplomacy in France in the time of Louis XIV. This school was in operation for only eight years, but very much later, after the War of 1870, it was the inspiration for l'Ecole Libre des Sciences Politiques d'Emile Boutmy. In the earlier school of the seventeenth century, students took special courses in international and public law. Their principal studies were in modern and diplomatic history (from the reign of Louis XII); they learned Italian, Spanish, Latin, and English. In the study of history, Père le Grand, the Director of the school, held the view that a student should be less interested in military campaigns than in the causes of war and in other events in the world of international affairs. Young diplomatic secretaries were also trained in the art of graceful expression, both spoken and written.

Baron de Szilassy, in his *Traité practique de la diplomatie moderne,* gave an interesting account of the technical knowledge required by officers of the foreign service. In his view, good diplomats, just as good lawyers, must master the technical aspects of their profession. In consequence, they must be familiar with international law and with the various international agreements, whether political or economic, which are in force between their own country and the country of their diplomatic mission. Furthermore, they must keep informed of other matters relevant to diplomacy; without being experts in everything, they must be sufficiently well informed to know where to find the precise information which they need. This authority observed, with a great deal of good sense, that candidates are sometimes required to learn a great deal which they will not in fact be called upon to use except much later in their careers. He adds, with a touch of malice, that if ministers and ambassadors had to pass, without warning, the competitive examinations, the results would not be invariably brilliant. If the candidates had the requisite qualities in other matters, he believed that it was quite enough for them to know a little diplomatic history. Too much importance, however, must not be attached to this subject, which is often only of very little practical use. He recommended also the study of international law, of political economy, and of the principles as well as the practices of international commerce.

Through this summary of the traditional authorities' views on the technical qualifications of foreign service officers, it is possible to emphasize the following conclusions: the principle has been established that the greatest importance must be attached to moral qualities and to wide scholarship; diplomats should have read in a wide variety of subjects and, in particular, they must be familiar with diplomatic history, international law, political economy and, above all, history. The classical writers are also unanimous in underlining the importance to diplomats of an ability to express themselves correctly and precisely, whether in speech or in writing.

This summary review of the classic treatises on the diplomat must be compared with the scale approved by the Civil Service Commission for grading the examinations. For example, in assigning a certain number of marks for international affairs, for history, or for prose composition, the Civil Service Commission and the Department determine the list and the degree of importance of the various qualities considered essential for officers of our foreign service. It is of some interest to note that in general the procedures followed by the Commission and by the Department conform almost exactly to the suggestions proposed by the traditional authorities.

The practices followed by the Department to obtain observations on the work and on the merits of its officers provide further corroboration. The qualities which are particularly valued in officers of the Department and which lead to promotion are identical with those which are taken into account in choosing the candidates in the first place. This question will be considered in greater detail in the next chapter.

So much for theory.

To put it to the test, we undertook a study of the career in the Department of one of our diplomats at each of the successive levels to determine the skills and the special qualities which they had been able to demonstrate. In each case we selected for the test the most brilliant subject. Now this study has shown that these same qualities which have seemed important to authorities on diplomacy over the ages have been demonstrated by the young diplomats who have been particularly successful in our Department.

With this same objective still in mind, that is, to define the qualities indispensable to a foreign service officer, let us set aside all theoretical notions and limit our inquiry to an analysis of the work entrusted to a young diplomatic secretary immediately upon his arrival in Ottawa; let us inquire what are the funds of knowledge and the skills which in practice are essential to him if he is to master his duties.

In Ottawa, a capable secretary studies the files systematically; he reads them analytically; he prepares minutes on them and decides what action to take, if action is appropriate. Thus he is capable of deciding, in dealing with any question, what files should be created. In brief, a young secretary possesses some experience and some idea of the organization of the work of the office.

In addition, however, to knowing how to set up and use a filing system, the secretary is responsible for the correspondence relative to the subject matters of his files; that is to say, he is competent to draft letters to the public or to other departments. His style is clear, simple, and precise. He possesses enough judgment and good sense to know the limits of his competence. He decides what questions must be referred to his immediate superior, to the Deputy Minister, to the Minister, or even to the Cabinet. To carry out his work effectively, the secretary thus needs to understand the organization of his own Department and the responsibilities of the various other departments. Thus, he must possess some knowledge of constitutional law, and of administrative regulations and procedures.

The secretary also drafts memoranda for heads of division and for the Minister. These memoranda set out a problem clearly, proposing appropriate decisions. The secretary knows how to draft despatches and telegrams. Whatever the question, he knows the exact limit of his own authority, and if special authorization is required, he submits the point at issue to the competent authorities or services, in the established terms.

During his period of service in Ottawa, a young secretary attends meetings and is responsible for the minutes. Sometimes he is called upon to prepare the agenda and later to draft the correspondence and the memoranda which may be necessary to make effective the decisions reached during the meeting. Now and then in these interdepartmental meetings the secretary may be called upon to express the views of his Department; and he must express what he has to say briefly and clearly.

To perform the duties assigned to him in Ottawa, it is apparent that to be successful a young secretary should have the following abilities: his language must be correct, whether in speech or in writing; he must have some knowledge of administration; he must know how policies are developed both within his Department and in the Government (this implies, as observed above, some knowledge of constitutional law and administrative procedures); he must have some knowledge of Canadian foreign policies and of the factors which influence them.

He must know also, once a policy has been determined, how the Department and the missions abroad are responsible for making it effective.

In the course of his duties abroad, as noted in previous chapters, a secretary drafts reports or memoranda on conversations he may have with citizens of the country of his mission or with visiting Canadians. He follows the consular and administrative regulations which guide the operations of our missions. From time to time, the young secretary prepares press reviews and undertakes research projects at the request of the head of mission or, it may be, of his immediate superior. The young secretary serves also as office manager in the smaller posts. He supervises and maintains the conduct of the mission's work. The competent secretary is, moreover, fully qualified, as also observed earlier, to make studies of political and economic conditions in the country of his mission and to prepare regular reports on these various subjects for the information of the Department. Usually, he does the consular work and provides information about Canada. Thus, to carry out his work abroad, a young secretary must have some knowledge of international law, of diplomatic history, of research work, of the arts and letters of his own country and of the country where he is posted, of sources of information and their relative importance, of the running of the registry, of the foreign policies of the country where he is serving and of the influences which may shape them.

For our definition of the competent diplomatic secretary, four different sources—the traditional authorities, the scale of examination marks, the careers of our ablest diplomats, the nature of the work to be done—give us consistent suggestions. The qualities of a competent secretary can be reduced in the main to the following five essentials:

1. A thorough university training and some specialist knowledge of Canadian and international affairs. But even more important than purely academic knowledge is the intellectual discipline resulting from these studies, a receptive mind trained to develop objective conclusions, able to master a complex subject and to draw from it a precise fund of information.
2. Good judgment, that is to say, skill in isolating practicable conclusions, in using theoretical knowledge or factual information obtained by scientific methods.
3. Precision, organization, effectiveness. The foreign service officer is a servant of the Government and must possess the qualities of a capable administrator.
4. An unusual capacity for expression. The competent officer of the Department must know how to express his ideas, whether orally or written, gracefully. In Ottawa, he is an adviser to the Government; his opinions and his recommendations must be set forth clearly and logically. Abroad, the foreign service officer is the observer and the representative of the Canadian Government. For the purposes of the Department, his worth is largely judged by his ability to express himself with exactness in written communications.
5. Personal and moral qualities. This point need not be laboured. The competent secretary has an easy, natural manner; he is adaptable; he is versatile

enough to live in foreign countries without too much difficulty.

This account has been a little long and complicated, but it will be readily understood why it has been considered necessary if it is remembered that this analysis of the qualities and of the skills of a young secretary is the foundation for our competitive examinations; it thus establishes a definition of the Canadian diplomat in the precise context of his administrative duties.

The competitive examinations for admission to the Department have been constituted to conform to a logically developed idea of the young Canadian diplomat. No claim is made that all our officers possess to an exceptional degree all the qualities discussed above; but it is useful, or so we believe, that those who have in mind a diplomatic career as well as those who study the course of our diplomacy know in general the professional ideal which our profession set as its objective in creating the means for its growth, and for its continuing renewal.

Here, then, are the criteria for selection on the personal and technical levels. But is must not be forgotten that Canada is a country of two cultures; if our diplomatic service professes to be properly representative, it must reflect this fundamental fact. How, then, can we manage to recruit a suitable proportion of French-speaking Canadians?

There is clearly a choice among three procedures: two separate examinations, a single examination, or a compromise. The procedure of holding two different examinations was abandoned for two reasons: first, the basic requirements of the profession are identical in spite of any difference in language, and since, during the course of their careers, officers are in competition for promotion, they must not be recruited by different standards to avoid any prejudice against those who have had an easier entrée into the Department. On the other hand, the system of a single competition does not take into account the fact that, although candidates must be equipped to carry out the same duties, they have not had the same training and in consequence should not be subject to the same criteria of selection. The procedure adopted, therefore, had to take into account both the professional demands of the Department, which are uniform, and the varied nature of the candidates' training. Thus, at the various stages of the competition, this fact is taken into account in setting for French-speaking candidates special questions of the same degree of difficulty as those which are designed for English-speaking candidates.

Clearly, there cannot be two methods of interpreting clauses of the Canadian constitution, an English and a French method, or two standards of loyalty and of honesty. It follows, therefore, that a certain kind of question and of test must be directed or applied to all candidates, without distinction. But if it is desired to test their intellectual interests, it is not fair to expect, for example, that French-speaking candidates should know as much as their English-speaking colleagues about Toynbee or Henry Moore. The same objective is reached, however, in asking them questions on Grousset or Maillol. A question concerning Shakespeare could have its complement in another question on Racine, leaving the choice to the candidates. The same procedure is valid for the oral examination. Examiners must know how to adapt their judgments to the differences in intellectual approach, to the peculiar orientation of the candidates, while maintaining the same level of excellence. The competition should not result in the selection of candidates identical in every respect from all regions of our country, but should aim at a balance between the qualities of the young officers who within the Department will later on represent the principal linguistic and cultural elements of Canada.

As for class distinctions, in many countries the requirement of private means to maintain an appropriate social position, since salaries were very modest, eliminated for a very long time all those who did not belong to the landed aristocracy or, later on, to the aristocracy of industry or finance. In a democratic country such as Canada, where class distinctions are still not strongly marked, it would have been a gross error to have adopted similar procedures. It has therefore been necessary to set salaries and allowances at a level which would permit officers otherwise qualified but without private means to carry out their work with reasonable ease of mind in money matters. Individual worth rather than family resources has determined departmental recruiting; the result has been that there has developed, in the composition and in the attitudes of the Department, a democratic character of the finest quality. Other countries have often noted this fact, and to our credit; in Ottawa, in departmental circles, just as in our embassies abroad, private means have only their appropriate place, a place, that is to say, subordinate and secondary.

For some little time during a period which we might call the constitutional or the imaginative, the Department attracted intellectuals, university professors for example, and experts in constitutional law. There grew up around Dr. Skelton[2] a team, a brains trust, concerned rather with the constitutional evolution of the country within the Commonwealth than with the perfection of a precise system of reporting. As the diplomatic service developed, experts in administration and other officers with a well-developed sense of the practical were required along with the theoreticians. For this reason, in our service as in all diplomatic services, from now on there will no longer be room only for the theoretician; administrative ability and a knowledge of the practical will be equally necessary.

Personal and professional worth, an ability to represent the varied cultural elements of our country, an attachment to democracy, a sense of the practicable—these are components characteristic of the image of our diplomatic officers, as conceived by the Department.

[2]Dr. O. D. Skelton, formerly professor of political science at Queen's University, was the Under-Secretary of State for External Affairs from 1925 until his death in 1941. The brains trust which he gathered about him included, among others, Mr. Norman Robertson, Mr. L. B. Pearson, Mr. R. B. Bryce, Mr. J. W. Pickersgill, Mr. Pierre Dupuy, the late Mr. Jean Désy, and Mr. Jules Léger. This is by no means the entire list, but those mentioned above made distinguished careers for themselves, whether in External Affairs or in other departments of Government.

8

Promotions

CERTAIN ASPECTS of the Department's system of promotion also throw light upon the character of the Canadian diplomat. Promotion policies, moreover, are matters of the greatest importance for the proper working of the service. If these policies are wisely determined, they encourage among officers of the Department a bent for hard work and for initiative, through the stimulus of ambition; on the other hand, from the departmental point of view, they guide through successive stages to responsible positions those who are best qualified, that is to say, those who alone can undertake competently the direction of affairs, and ultimately serve as ready replacements for officers holding the more important positions.

First of all, promotions must be determined within the context of the financial policies of the Government. If there were no limit to parliamentary funds and if every deserving effort could be recognized in financial terms, the organization of a system of promotions would present no difficulties. But in the administration of Canadian affairs, before an officer can be promoted, it is not enough to convince the Civil Service Commission that the duties of an officer have grown to the point where an increase in salary is warranted; it still remains essential that funds be available, within the limitations of the Government's financial policies. Thus, it can happen that during a period of rigid economy a deserving officer may see his promotion delayed, or even endangered. It is, of course, theoretically true that a well-qualified officer could be asked to transfer to another governmental service where he might have an unrestricted and better-paid appointment; but these transfers from one department to another occur rarely, and with difficulty; the various departments of government have limited rewards to offer to their own employees, and more often than not they naturally do what they can to reserve for their own officers the few positions which may become available in their establishments.

In addition to purely financial considerations, there are others which delay promotion. In principle, irrespective of their merits, officers can expect promotion only every two years, for the very good reason that there are only six or seven grades in the diplomatic service before the rank of Ambassador is reached; and if unusual ability were the only factor taken into consideration, an exceptionally gifted officer could reach the summit of his career when not much more than thirty years of age. When the probable extent of our approved establishment in the next ten or fifteen years is taken into account, and the higher posts which will then be available, the rate of promotion

for even the best-qualified officers must be restrained.
There must not be a congestion of candidates at the
higher levels through premature promotions. It is thus
seen that promotion can be delayed for financial reasons
or for administrative purposes in a manner not fully
consistent with absolute justice.

In accordance with principles established by the Civil
Service Commission, promotion is granted essentially
on a basis of merit; but in the Department of External
Affairs, the problem of determining the relative merit of
officers becomes complicated in that they are scattered
throughout the world, and that the heads of mission,
sometimes nominated from outside the service, are not
invariably able to make comparable judgments on the
work of their juniors. To limit the dangers involved in this
dispersion of our officers, the rating of officers has been
divided into two operations: the estimates placed upon
officers by the heads of mission or of division and, in
Ottawa, the collation of the assigned ratings to establish
priority lists for the promotion of officers at each level.

The basis for the estimate which the heads of mission
must make on each officer is a scale set, like the competitive examination for admission, in terms of the
Department's estimate of the qualities essential to a competent officer.

It has often been considered whether these personal
reports should be made known to the officers. The few
experiments in doing this have emphasized the fact that
ratings become singularly more flattering, and less useful,
if the officers concerned know about them. This is easily
explained. In a small mission—and most of our missions
are small—relationships between the head of mission
and his assistant are very close. Their work as a team

becomes impossible if the junior officer comes to know that his head of mission will be sending home an unfavourable report about him. The junior officer may perhaps give certain undertakings, and in consequence the head of mission will change his report; but it may happen that these intentions are not in fact made good. Furthermore, a head of mission normally does not like to discourage a junior officer. Even when an unfavourable report is justified, a head of mission will be reluctant to make it if he knows that his junior officer will find out about it, and will probably bear a grudge. To maintain an atmosphere of goodwill within our missions and to avoid weakening the system of objective ratings, an absolute essential, the Department has provisionally adopted a different procedure. The heads of mission do not have the right to make an adverse report upon an officer unless they have warned him in good time of his weaknesses and unless, in finally making the report, they have warned him for the second time that, since he has not been able to amend or to better his ways, he cannot expect to be given a favourable one. In consequence, officers know that failing notice to the contrary their services are satisfactory, and that they have no reason to fear adverse comments. They are also aware that if everything is not going satisfactorily they will be warned, and that an adverse report upon them will not be prepared before they have had a reasonable opportunity to get things in hand.

The second phase in establishing the rating of officers takes place within the Department in Ottawa. The Department, in brief, compares reports from the various heads of mission on officers of the same class, and tries to establish a priority list for promotions. The members of the Promotions Committee rate or review the evaluations. In this manner the collective experience of the Department comes to bear upon the proposed evaluations, and results in practice in a series of ratings for each class of officer which is used, along with age and seniority, to determine the promotions of the current year. As time goes on, the judgments relevant to each officer become more detailed and more precisely graduated, and, most important, they finally result in classifications increasingly searching and objective for all officers, in the order of their abilities.

The question, of course, arises of determining in what precisely consist the virtues which warrant promotion and serve as a basis for the system of evaluation. This rating mark is substantially in conformity with the standards which served in the selection of the candidates at the competitive examinations; the criteria detailed in the preceding chapter appear again with, of course, appropriate emphasis on results thus far evident, and on expectations for the future, particularly for officers of the higher ranks.

The system for promotions must also take into account the dual nature of our service. The problem is not peculiar to our Department; it arises within all branches of the administration. It is quite apparent that if the various services are planned and organized exclusively by English-speaking Canadians, French-Canadian officers who obtain promotion will be those who possess or who will know how to acquire most quickly the spirit, the methods, and, above all, the language of their English-speaking colleagues. By a curious paradox, there will be a tendency to regard the least typically French-Canadian officers as the most useful officers. And unless precautions are taken, the system of promotion by merit could result in a stimulus to become completely anglicized.

Great care must be taken on the one hand not to demand for French-Canadian officers the creation of a system of promotions which would in fact apply to them different criteria. There are not two ways of being loyal, conscientious, exact, moderate, courteous, or prudent. Is it not apparent that somehow there must be applied, for the public good and the efficiency of the administration, criteria consistently valid whatever the mother tongue of the officer? This much said, we hasten to add that officers responsible for passing judgment on French Canadians must bear in mind that for some time at least difficulties with English and with administrative methods in Ottawa can affect their work. These officers must also remember that a French Canadian will not have the same attitude toward his work as they do, and that his methods will inevitably be different. They must be able to remember that only the final result is important. It is to be expected that French Canadians will not always show the same preferences as their English-speaking compatriots for certain duties. Fundamental differences of temperament and of aptitude must be recognized and must be used to enrich the public service in the necessarily varied duties which are its responsibility; there must be no insistence that French Canadians conform to one and only one standard which will necessarily be alien to their mentality and will make it impossible for them either to be dealt justice in promotion, or to deal justly with the administration by serving it to the limit of their powers. The time has now arrived in the administration to take precautions against what could amount to an indirect method of anglicizing, no doubt without intent, our French-Canadian officers; this does in fact raise a strong obstacle to their recruitment and to their promotion alike. French Canadians can take a useful and unique part in the administration while remaining loyal to the spirit of their race. To this there must be no inadvertent barrier.

Within the Department of External Affairs, officers at all levels are well aware of the difficulties to which this problem gives rise, and at all stages in the rating of officers great pains are taken to do justice to a compatriot of a different tongue. Moreover, it is now an established practice to have a French Canadian as deputy minister or associate deputy minister. He takes part in the meetings on ratings and promotions; his colleagues call him into conference on the evaluations given to his French-speaking brothers; and if, in addition, the head of the Personnel Division is a French Canadian (as I was, for a period of several years), it is quite clear that French Canadians have only themselves to blame if their special qualities are not recognized.

We have tackled this delicate problem, first of all to recognize its existence and to indicate its extent, and further because we are happy to pay tribute to the genuinely Canadian spirit animating our English-speaking colleagues in the Department.

There is a further interesting point in this matter of promotions, that is, their publication. The Department announces regularly its promotion lists. Thus, every officer knows exactly where he stands in the lists in relation to his colleague. This decision to make promotions public was deliberately taken to encourage those who are not promoted to ask themselves the reasons for this setback in their careers. Their questions and, on, occasion, protests make it possible to bring the matter out into the open and to provide an opportunity of pointing out to them why they are not making progress. Naturally, this task is the responsibility of the Personnel Division; there are indeed more agreeable tasks, but if our officers are prepared to be reasonable, they will know at least in what direction they must concentrate their efforts to better their chances of promotion. It is particularly important that they know that promotions are not handed out without their knowledge, or without their having an opportunity to make their case and to draw attention to their abilities, if this is appropriate. Thanks to this practice of publication, profitable discussions can be held with officers who, in all good faith, are unaware of their shortcomings; in addition, interesting exchanges of views take place on the characters and on the prejudices of certain heads of mission. This evidence is not lost to view when the ratings which they send in come up for review in the following year.

There must also be emphasized the progressive nature of our officers' careers; they do not enter the government service to remain indefinitely in a posting as third secretary. It is of the very essence of the hiring contract that the officer will advance in rank, and that ultimately he will become Minister or Ambassador. There do not therefore exist two distinct categories of officers in the Canadian diplomatic service, specialists recruited on their merits and posted to executive duties, and, on the other hand, friends of the Government in power posted to planning and supervisory duties. The Canadian diplomatic service is based rather upon a uniform system which permits a gifted officer to proceed from rank to rank, right to the highest responsibilities. In this respect our service differs widely both from other branches of the public service (normally more static), and from certain other diplomatic services.

Selected on a merit system, graded according to his abilities and his energies, the Canadian diplomat gives an impression of earnestness, of industry, of some self-consciousness, perhaps, but of genuine and strong devotion to the public service. The system of promotion which he shares again suggests characteristics of his mentality and nature: respect for objectivity, moderation, a zeal to protect the young against discrimination by seniors, and receptiveness to the contribution which the minority group can bring; like the functions of the Department and its methods of work, these characteristics seem to us to be significant.

9
The Diplomat as a Civil Servant

THE DIPLOMAT, as we have observed, is a civil servant; but travel abroad and work in other countries make of him a special kind of civil servant. It is by no means certain that the public in general realizes what is involved in the conduct of public business in distant and foreign countries.

The normal civil servant is more or less permanently installed in one place. The diplomat, for his part, must move his household treasures more or less regularly every three years. This displacement is not a simple matter of moving within his own country, for often enough he must cross the oceans and the continents. He looks about, naturally, for a place to live immediately upon his arrival, when everything is strange and unfamiliar to him. He discovers, usually too late, that the tenant in some countries pays the taxes; that he must make an inventory of his living quarters before moving in—otherwise, at the end of the lease he must pay for the wear and tear of all his predecessors. He cannot, moreover, move in anywhere at all, since his house has an official status and must be suitable for giving receptions.

Occasionally, particularly when a new mission is established, and this arises especially in a new service such as ours, he must in addition find quarters for professional duties, the offices of the chancellory and the residence of the head of mission. In Canada, it is not an easy matter for one to find a place to live; it is much more difficult abroad; and when provision must also be made for professional duties, the problem becomes further complicated. It is obviously necessary also to find a select part of the city, a reasonable price, the necessary number of rooms—no more than that—and then try to persuade the Treasury Board several thousand miles away; and in the meantime, the owner is not at all indisposed to change his mind.

Having once arranged for his private and official quarters, the foreign service officer plies his trade in conditions quite different from those prevalent in Canada. He recruits local employees, supervises the running of the office, and carries out his own normal duties, giving accounts of his activities to heads of division who seem as remote as the other end of the world, and who cannot always, in spite of their goodwill, understand local conditions. In Ottawa, if a secretary requests promotion, his chief telephones the head of Personnel Division, and the thing is done. Abroad, he must write, and he must explain. In Ottawa, a civil servant may need chairs; he discusses this with the administrative services, and knows the situation at once. If he is abroad, he must write, explaining the why and the wherefore, and then wait. In brief, the officer abroad encounters all the difficulties of a civil servant who must get on with his work and, in addition, give accounts from far away to the administrative authorities at home.

Living conditions and the methods of work are different. The working day, the holidays, the procedures to be followed are unfamiliar. Sometimes there are months of delay in getting a reply to a casual inquiry. Simple statistical information is often not available. In Canada, to have a valise taken to a hotel room, the amount of the tip is fixed; abroad, there are often surprises. At home, a telephone call is often enough to get an answer to a question; in other countries, to get the same information it is sometimes necessary to invite the competent official for a drink, or for dinner. Furthermore, the altitude or the climate can be trying. Not unusually the local food is dangerous, and an officer is sometimes ill one day out of three. It would be easy to give further illustrations; but it is already apparent to what degree the life of the civil servant-diplomat can be complicated because of his move abroad, through his remoteness and through differences in living conditions.

In Canada, a civil servant is expected to give the greatest possible co-operation to his fellow officers, whether of the same service or of a different branch of the administration. Civil servants of other governments, however, naturally do not feel under the same obligation toward a representative of Canada. Hence stems the need that a foreign service officer, if he wishes to get on with his work, establish cordial personal relations with people of the local administration who can help him; the less effective the local administration, the more important these friendly connections.

If the diplomat has only to maintain relationships between his own and the local government, he could limit his contacts abroad to civil servants. But he must also obtain information, he must make Canada better known, and stimulate trade. In consequence, he must extend his relationships to include all kinds of groups and institutions which can have some bearing on the various fields of his own activities. But he must not wait until a crisis arises to enter into these relationships; he must take appropriate action in advance, so that if his duties require it he may call upon or receive a call from someone capable of providing him with what he needs.

He must possess not only adequate resources but special personal capacities and a certain measure of the social graces not generally required of civil servants in their professional capacities. Many civil servants in Canada can get on with their work even if they are hard to get along with or do not ever give a reception. The foreign service officer lacking in social resourcefulness and in amiable qualities is bound to fail.

While the civil servant in Canada must normally make it his business to become a member of a team responsible for certain services provided for by law, the Canadian civil servant abroad will the better discharge his duties to the extent that he will not limit himself to being only a civil servant, but will know how to become an active and popular member of the local society, whether diplomatic or not. And in this field his personal gifts and the hospitality of his home are important factors which normally do not have any counterpart in the life of the civil servant in Canada. Further, the diplomat's knowledge of the language and of the culture of the country where he is serving is obviously a matter of great consequence to him. In this too he is different from his colleagues in other branches of the administrative services who are not usually called upon, for professional reasons, to master several languages and to be familiar with the culture of foreign countries.

In Canada, the civil servant belongs to a specific service, and his interests are confined almost entirely to problems of his own department. This is by no means true for the diplomatic officer; when he is abroad he must be concerned with the problems and become an officer of all the services of the Government. Where there is no military or commercial attaché, for example, the foreign service officer must take on their functions whenever the Department of National Defence or Trade and Commerce require some service or other, or wish to obtain information. In the small missions (most of our missions are small), the secretary in turn represents Immigration for visa matters, Citizenship to register a birth, or the Post Office to conduct a special negotiation. Again, in information, the officer abroad does not limit his interests to matters of foreign policy; he deals with all the requests for information which may come to him, and he is called upon to give details on educational institutions, agriculture, climate, sports, and so on.

Thus, during the course of his career, the diplomat naturally is drawn to interests in all aspects of Canadian life. All services of the Government, of course, cannot be represented in all our missions abroad. When the extent of business does not justify the appointment of a special representative of a department in a country abroad, that department must rely upon the foreign

service officer on each occasion when it desires some
task on the part of the mission. It is not surprising, therefore, if the diplomat, knowing as he must his own particular field of foreign affairs, is not at the same time the
universal expert which each governmental service would
like him to become in entrusting their affairs to him. It
is true that, if a matter is of sufficient importance, the
Government occasionally sends out an expert negotiator;
but, even so, the diplomat is still indispensable to give
advice on the best way of conducting business and on the
appropriate people to approach; the diplomat's knowledge
of the milieu will be of great service to the expert and
will permit him to take action, fully informed of local
conditions.

Differing from many other civil servants, the diplomat
is essentially a student of affairs, an adviser rather than
an executive or an administrative officer. Of course,
when he is abroad, he must issue visas, take action to get
Canadians out of trouble, and conduct negotiations according to the instructions he receives; but more often
he applies his energies to discover the underlying meaning
of events, and to determine in what way these may have
an influence upon us; he is the adviser on the best method
to adopt in order to attain the desired results in any given
circumstance. He cannot discharge his duties if he has
not first of all devoted a good deal of time to the study
of the milieu, if he is not already familiar with it. His
trade is to try to know what is happening and, on occasion, to know what may or will likely happen. No doubt
because of his duty to be on the alert to what is going on
precisely at the moment when things are hardly stirring,
at just that moment when hardly anything appears above
the surface, a diplomat earns the reputation for intrigue

and for sinister secrets which is often given him. This is, of course, in part an exaggeration; but it remains true that the competent diplomat must be exceedingly knowing to do his work effectively.

Whether in fact the business at hand is to negotiate, or to stimulate trade, or to get a Canadian tourist out of trouble, is it not apparent that a knowledge of the milieu and of its people will be a matter of decisive importance for the diplomat? The diplomat is not entirely bound to his office. To become familiar with the country where he is on mission, he must travel, he must attend debates in parliament, and he must follow important law cases; his interests must be general, in the arts and in the economic life of the country just as much as in political events. A scientific discovery can have, as we know all too well, military consequences and international implications. A poem can mark a turning-point in the thinking of a group and foretell a development with important tangible results. Everything has its importance in the life of a nation; the diplomat is alert to the slightest symptoms indicating a probable direction of development. In brief, he tries to understand the spirit of the people who are his hosts, a spirit which will be revealed at all times as self-consistent and essentially unchanging in matters which are of concern to Canada. Even everyday sights in the streets will be a source of information to the diplomat in that they will disclose to him something of a people's mentality, impulsive and not to be restrained.

The diplomat, moreover, is a civil servant of a very special kind. He is concerned with problems of other departments, and in order to understand the country where he is on duty he must study it in all its aspects and examine every sort of question which may arise. Nor-

mally, civil servants have more precisely defined fields
of activity; if they are professionally trained, they usually
work in their specialized fields. But the diplomat cannot
be only an engineer or a lawyer or a historian. It is desirable that he should have advanced technical training;
but to carry out his duties he must also be able to judge
and to understand the activities of all the professions
and of an entire nation, and to make of them an ap-
prehensible whole, if he is to practise his profession adequately—to keep the Canadian Government well informed, to conduct negotiations, and to protect Canadian
interests most effectively.

The foreign service officer, therefore, must adapt himself to conditions different from those he may have known
in Canada; he must know how to establish useful relationships and to be concerned with matters lying within
the competence of other departments. In other words,
he must be versatile, and he must not be disturbed by an
unsettled life, or by the unexpected. But all these preoccupations form only one side of his profession; his real
interests stem from the fact that he must come to know
the very heart of a people, to interpret the forces which
drive it towards its particular destiny; if he is successful
in this task, the diplomat sometimes succeeds in understanding how these forces may be brought into harmony
with the interests and with the noblest ambitions of his
own country. This high purpose, a purpose sometimes
forgotten, gives him comfort for the better-known mis-
fortunes of a profession familiar enough with misfortune.
But in thus devoting himself to the highest interests of
his country, it must be added at once, the diplomat is no
longer different from his fellows, from other servants of
the state who in their own spheres pursue the same ideal.

It is seen, then, that usually the activities of the civil servant-diplomat have a character more varied and, as will be seen in detail in the following chapter, more hazardous than that of other servants of the state. The old cliché of the civil servant submerged in routine and in his petty rounds no longer is relevant to the demands imposed by the life of a Canadian diplomat.

The organization of the service also clarifies certain essential characteristics of the Canadian diplomat. He is a civil servant; that is to say, he is recruited in terms of the law which governs the entire civil service and he is subject to the demands and to the responsibilities required of any Canadian civil servant. He receives his salary, for example, only if he is in fact present and on duty at his posting; it would be quite wrong to believe that, far from the eye of the home administration, he can travel about or be at liberty as he sees fit. In this respect his official life is in fact somewhat rigid, a rigidity not imposed on services where the staff is not recruited on a basis of merit and is not subject to the normal regulations of the civil service.

Belonging as he does to a service anxious to be homogeneous and effective, the Canadian diplomat will move about more and will be entrusted with new duties perhaps more often than his colleagues in other services, even in Canadian services such as those of Trade and Commerce and of Immigration, for example, which leave their officers in the same postings for much longer periods, and often, it may be, indefinitely.

As an officer of a service of modest size, he will, moreover, be unable to become a specialist except in the principles and in the methods of his profession; in this he is different not only from officers of more extensive diplomatic services, but also from other civil servants who ultimately become real experts and, at times, the sole counsellors of the Government in the areas assigned to them.

As a member of a new governmental service, the Canadian diplomat is still seeking his way. He has not yet discovered the final formula for organization and homogeneity; in the countries where we have diplomatic missions, he sometimes is still proceeding tentatively to discover the real scope of our interests, and the nature and the purpose of the relationships which can be formed between Canada and the country of his posting. In brief, the Canadian Department of External Affairs is still at an exploratory stage; there is still some sense of strain, an atmosphere of a research laboratory; for our officers this provides a valued stimulus, but at the same time it leads to difficulties which must not be ignored. Canadian diplomacy, like any youngster, is still wondering how it will finally look.

10
The Rough with the Smooth

THE PROFESSIONS of the lawyer, the doctor, or the teacher ultimately leave their mark upon them. This is equally true for the diplomat—his profession leaves upon him familiar scars.

Everyone is familiar with the classic portrait of a diplomat: meticulously dressed, restrained in speech, punctilious in social relationships, at ease in any company, a man of the world, resourceful, even somewhat crafty, often cynical or at least mildly sceptical, little given to enthusiasm—in brief, remote, refined, but, taken all together, oddly ripe for caricature, not a lovable person.

It would be all too easy to claim that this is a false portrait, and to demonstrate point by point that in fact the real-life diplomat or the Canadian diplomat is an entirely different person. It would be easy but useless. It

is our intention rather to determine what there may be
that is inevitable in certain features of the diplomatic
character, if he bows to the demands of his profession.
Once alerted to the perils lurking for him in certain
imperatives of his profession, he can more readily be on
his guard against them; if he is not successful, we can
perhaps be more indulgent toward his weaknesses if we
realize that these are wounds he has suffered in the service
of his country.

Beyond any doubt, the diplomat who is not on guard
tends to become superficial. Since he moves from one
country to another every three or four years, unless he
is alert he may in truth end by having no roots anywhere. His ability, if he has any, is rapidly enmeshed in
protocol and in formalities; he knows the orders of pre-
cedence; he knows the proper procedure for presenting
letters of credence, and he knows what visits must be
made; he is familiar with the refinements of innumerable
diplomatic formulas, and he makes knowing use of them.
This special knowledge is to diplomacy what grammar is
to literature; it is difficult to get along without it, but it is
by no means enough to provide a full life.

The diplomat and his Department can take precautions against this tendency. First, as for Canada, diplomatic officers must almost of necessity spend their time
partly abroad and partly in Ottawa in tours of duty of
three or four years. This means that normally an officer is
not away from his country for more than four years, and
that half of his career is spent in Ottawa.

Moreover, he may, if he wishes, specialize in one or
another of the subject-matters which are basic to diplo-
cacy: economics, law, or, again, a region or a particular
continent. Thus, he can fight off the danger of becoming

a smatterer and can acquire, if he so wishes, a genuine competence in a field which gives him a part in the vital interests of his country.

This is equally true in his social obligations. The diplomat clearly must entertain a good deal and have an active social life. He can easily enough, in the various countries where he is briefly stationed, be content with maintaining relationships with important people who have some official duty, or who should be cultivated for the purposes of his work. By adhering to this system he can even achieve a considerable social success, particularly if he knows how to manage this matter on a sound basis of snobbery. But if the right stuff is in him, he will take a genuine interest in the problems of the country which is his host; his profession obliges him to discover the inner workings of a country's political life and of its foreign policies. This work, to a large extent, he can do in his own office, but to do it really well he must know those who are in the forefront of each field, those who are in one way or another identified with the problems which he is studying. The relationships with these people, established on the level of personal friendships, are not of a kind which he can lay aside like a cloak when he leaves the country. In fact, his duties demand of him and also give him the opportunity to establish relationships with the most distinguished philosophers and men of affairs. If he really respects his profession, his relationships with them will be by no means superficial, quite the contrary, and his own culture and his own apprehension of problems of all kinds will in consequence be deeply affected.

In all countries and at all times servants of the government are poorly paid. Must the Canadian diplomat as a

civil servant take the vow of poverty? In actual fact, in
his profession anxieties about money, a new element—
diplomats of other years very often had ample personal
resources—are not of a kind to cripple his activities. It
is indeed true that diplomatic life is expensive, but since
the recruiting of our officers must be done on a democratic basis, the state has grown used to paying their
expenses abroad without excessive surliness.

The official duty of a diplomat is to represent the state
abroad, and the Treasury Board, graciously or not,
grants him about what he needs. Undoubtedly, as observed earlier, the diplomat has at times to give reasons,
to provide information which may seem to him useless
or excessively detailed. It is none the less true that abroad,
all things considered, he generally lives a more spacious
life than at home. His representative duties, whatever
his rank, guarantee him a minimum standard. He profits
personally, he could not manage otherwise, from the
resources which the state puts at his disposal to make
his work easier. On the other hand, when he comes home
again, the diplomat shares once again the austere lot of
his fellow civil servants.

But is he not, as a servant of the Government, doomed
to keep silent, and does he not acquire because of his
profession an habitual reticence? Too much has been
said about diplomatic discretion. Of course, the diplomat
must be well informed; during the course of negotiations
he must keep silent, for obvious reasons. But in the
normal course of events the diplomat is by no means as
silent as the tomb, and it is not to his own interests invariably to hold his tongue. He learns by experience that on
his first arrival in a new country he must refrain from
speaking on anything and everything. This is not so much

through any anxiety to keep his impressions to himself but through native prudence, since, more often than not, first impressions are incomplete and deceptive. The diplomat reserves his judgment because he, too, knows that to understand is often to pardon—and his profession obliges him to understand everything. Confidential information given to him for his Government does not belong to him. On this he keeps silent, just as ministers of the Crown must not reveal Cabinet deliberations.

Unlike the civil servant in Ottawa, however, who must not say anything, the diplomat abroad must defend as often as he can do so usefully the actions and the conduct of his country and of his Government. In this he may employ a liberty of expression and take an initiative entirely exceptional for a civil servant. Very often also the diplomat who wants to obtain information must himself contribute something to the conversation; at times he must offer to exchange rather than invariably to elicit confidential information. If he is not prepared to discuss his own point of view, to reveal the results of his studies or of his observations, he will be quickly isolated and left to his own resources. The mean to be observed in such conversations is delicate, but an entirely negative attitude undoubtedly reduces the usefulness of a diplomat.

The career of a diplomat is also often subject to chance and is full of incident. A bachelor with his law degree does not necessarily become a lawyer because he has a scroll attesting his devotion to the law; he needs a few years to discover whether he can in fact win his cases. The same is true for a doctor; only after some time can he decide whether he can be an effective practitioner. But once their minds are easy on that score, their principal problem is solved; the lawyer or the doctor can estimate in advance his income five or ten years hence, he can buy a house and a summer place and arrange, years in advance, that his son will go to university. Their lives normally should continue in an easily foreseen direction. But for the diplomat the case is quite different; he must first of all become adjusted to the Department in Ottawa; if he goes abroad, he must learn a foreign language, and make entry into a new profession which sometimes must be practised in difficult circumstances. Four years later he returns to an entirely different kind of work in a Department which during his absence has almost completely changed its personnel. After a few years he must again set forth for another country, and again he must begin by learning another language. No summer place, no house, nothing certain for him to look forward to. Every now and then his life is completely changed, and in new circumstances he must continuously give new evidence of his abilities, and show that he is capable of anything that can be required of him. There cannot possibly be any valid comparison between the life of the normal professional man and that of the diplomat who begins his career as a specialist in international aviation, to become then the Secretary of our Embassy in Mexico, to come back again to Ottawa to deal with personnel or legal questions, preliminary to his departure as Chargé d'Affaires of a mission beyond the Iron Curtain. These movements to and fro, which are at times disturbing and make remote the substance of his university studies, ultimately make of him a specialist of quite another kind, and fit him to play his special part within the administration, as observed in the chapter on Specialization.

There is also office politics, endemic to all departments. This topic would not be noticed here had it not such great importance for diplomats that ultimately, beyond doubt, it leaves its special mark upon them.

As part of his profession, the diplomat tries to understand the workings of the minds and the motives of the people with whom he comes in contact. Character analysis ultimately becomes an essential part of his method of working; it is the diplomat's misfortune that in his relations with his colleagues he cannot free himself from the tyranny of this practice. In consequence, when two officers of the Department chat together, more often than not they end up by discussing the virtues, the weaknesses, and the defects of a colleague; and this incessant preoccupation with the assessment of colleagues finally produces within the Department a numbing atmosphere. Sooner or later, a desire to escape from this atmosphere adds to the attractions of a posting abroad, where the demands of day-to-day work absorb all an officer's energies, and where office politics and manoeuvres lose something of their sharpness.

But diplomats do not engage in this mutual analysis in a spirit of pure mischief. In the normal course of things, they must pass part of their life abroad where, separated one from the other, they maintain their contacts by correspondence. Whether they are in Ottawa or abroad, it is vital to them to be accurately familiar with the various aspects of the character and of the qualities of their correspondent so as to complement their understanding of how things are really going; this it is never possible to set forth in depth in official documents. A head of division in Ottawa needs to know whether the counsellor in one mission or another is a born enthusiast or whether he is habitually indolent in carrying on his work. The head of the Personnel Division will treat quite differently a recommendation for the promotion of a secretary if he knows that the head of mission is very sparing in his praises or, on the other hand, is inclined to exaggerate the merits of his junior officers. When officers know one another well, they find no need to give long explanations, and their work is thus made easier.

The interest taken by officers, however, in the character of their brothers in the service is also understandable because during their careers they must live, both in Ottawa and abroad, in a close familiarity rarely known to other civil servants. They must work for one another; they must be helpful and encouraging, and they must stick together: the better they know each other, the easier it is for them to combine their joint efforts so as to work together as a smooth-running, efficient machine. The counsellor or the head of chancery must know whether he can entrust research work or representational duties to a young secretary. A head of mission must get to know promptly the abilities and the shortcomings alike of his first secretary.

Those outside the service do not always realize that if it is true that diplomats seem to regard one another highly, they are also given to introspection with a never ending curiosity on the varied aspects of their characters; this critical process is not always so courteous or charitable as might be wished. This is, of course, one of the minor aspects of the profession, but it does have beyond doubt some influence upon the diplomat in his relations with the Department. As a general rule, excessive zeal in these character studies inspires in the diplomat a reverent awe of the opinion of the East Block, and, more often than not, a well-formed conviction that it is much simpler to make his abilities known to and to deserve the trust of a head of mission abroad than to attract the attention and find favour in the eyes of a score of bureaucrats in Ottawa.

This stock exchange of reputations maintained in Ottawa, if it may be so described, certainly has a bearing upon the chance of promotion, for the diplomat is comparable both to the professional in private practice and to civil servants of other departments, so far as promotion is concerned. The lawyer and the doctor who are industrious are able to become rich and renowned in their professions. The diplomat also, if he is both successful and lucky, gets ahead in his career. In our Canadian system, promotion presupposes merit; but merit alone is not enough. It is also required that the needs of the service become greater, that duties are more demanding, and that the state is prepared to pay higher salaries; otherwise, as we have seen, there is no promotion. The diplomatic career, moreover, is well supplied with young officers, and others not so young, who have plenty of talent and ambition, and who are anxious also to get ahead. But there is not always room for everyone; that is to say, the promotion of a diplomat too is a competitive affair, and it is subject to the strokes of chance familiar to professional and business men.

A Canadian diplomat can normally expect to become head of a mission; most of our diplomatic missions are directed by career officers. The Department, as a matter of fact, has at its disposal as many higher positions (equivalent to that of a deputy minister) as the Government is prepared to fill with career diplomats as heads of mission. Promotion is to this extent accelerated. The Canadian diplomatic officer has had so far an advantage in the privileged position which he enjoys in relation to other civil servants. Expectations for the future which the Department offers rather than immediate material advantages have thus far maintained the high standards of its recruiting.

Travel abroad, opportunities for promotion, varied duties, and the stimulus of competition create a psychological milieu peculiar to the Department. There is present also a certain tenseness, an uneasiness, which can be occasionally glimpsed beneath the unruffled exterior of the diplomat whose profession consists in a curious blending of freedom and of restraint, of the changing and of the stable, of splendour and of simplicity, of crests and hollows, of coming and going.

At times it is well to bear in mind the ideals which the Canadian diplomat has tried to serve before judging too unkindly the faults which he has not known how, or has been unable, to avoid.

Conclusion

IT IS NOW POSSIBLE, as we come to the end of this study
of the Canadian diplomat, to reach a few general conclusions on his spiritual qualities, and on the special
manners and methods he employs in the practice of his
profession.

Our diplomatic service, British in origin and tradition,
has acquired a distinctive quality through its empirical
working methods. Its officers are not, or at least are no
longer, only symbols of our political independence, now
firmly established for the future. Our officers now have
real and numerous tasks and they must now, more than
ever in the past, demonstrate their organizing ability and
their sense of the practical. Our diplomats, little given
to generalizations or to theory, are characterized rather
by restraint in their actions and by anxiety to find workable solutions for problems as they arise.

Since our country is dual in its culture and federal
in its constitution, since we have close relationships with
Britain and the United States and hold the rank of a

middle power, our diplomatic representatives cannot often take extreme positions or propose revolutionary solutions. By instinct and by the nature of things, they are specialists in compromise, specialists in workable solutions rather than in imposing and sensational proposals. It is no exaggeration to claim that if our diplomatic officers do not often attract attention by spectacular initiatives, their day-to-day activities can win for them a solid reputation, and assure for them a very real weight.

Abroad, the Canadian diplomat has retained his habits of hospitality and of kindness, characteristic of a new country. His scale of living is modest, and his conduct and his actions are deeply democratic. Without meaning to be critical of other diplomatic services, those who are familiar with diplomats recognize that the Canadian diplomat does not regard himself as above commercial matters; and he loses no opportunity to take an interest in his fellow citizens who come as visitors to the country of his posting.

By and large, if in a single word must be summed up the manner in which the Canadian diplomat works, the appropriate word is "completeness."

The Canadian diplomat is not and does not become a stranger to his own country. On the contrary, he returns at regular intervals for a tour of duty in the Department in Ottawa, and resumes contact with the hard facts of Canadian life. Moreover, he does not regard himself as a member of an exceptional service, set apart from the others. He is recruited by the Civil Service Commission, as are other servants of the Government; his promotion proceeds in accord with regulations approved by the Commission. When he comes home, the Canadian diplomat enjoys no special privileges whatsoever; he is upon exactly the same footing as all other servants of the Government.

It has also been pointed out that the Canadian diplomat normally is not a specialist. His work is carried out as a member of a team; in the course of his career he moves from one duty to another, and is thus required to demonstrate a versatility not expected of officers belonging to a larger governmental service. His ability to move from one field to another does lead him, however, to take a broader view of the needs and activities of the service as a whole, and tends over the years to prepare him for supervisory and co-ordinating duties which in essence are those of a diplomat.

In the conduct of his work, the Canadian diplomat must give evidence of unquestionable ability. He is recruited and promoted on a basis of merit. Opportunities arise for him to give evidence of his capacities in varied circumstances; and he must, if he is to be successful, reveal unusual qualities of analysis, of judgment, and of good sense. Private means or distinguished birth alone are not, as in other diplomatic services, any guarantee of success.

The Canadian diplomat is not possessed of all the virtues of his country. It appears, however, possible, in consequence of this analytical study, to apprehend in him many characteristics which are unmistakably Canadian.